Dedicated to the servicemen and women
who bravely defended
our country and freedom
—at home and abroad—
during the dark days of World War II.
They pulled together to victory.
We pay our respects.

———————◼———————

MY FOLKS AND WORLD WAR II

A Treasury of World War II Stories
Shared By Capper's and Grit Readers

Capper Press
Topeka, Kansas

Editors
Marge Nichols Sullivan
Samantha Adams

Assistant to the Editors
Patricia Patterson Thompson

Production
Bruce Bealmear

Illustration
Stephen B. Falls

Copyright © 1994
by Capper Press
Printed in the United States of America

ISBN: 0-941678-43-1

FOREWORD

More than an end to war, we want
an end to the beginnings of all wars.
Franklin D. Roosevelt

The year was 1941. Americans had begun to recover from the hardships of the Great Depression, but an even more urgent crisis loomed on the horizon. For two years we had watched in horror as fascism and Nazism destroyed the hard-earned peace of World War I. America had not yet been drawn into the fray, but on December 7, everything would change.

With the unforgettable attack on Pearl Harbor, America plunged headlong into World War II. This book is a collection of personal experiences and family lore that *Capper's* and *Grit* readers have shared about the heroes who sacrificed and the folks who pulled together — at home and abroad — to win the War To End All Wars.

My Folks And World War II is the sixth volume in the *My Folks* series: *My Folks Came In A Covered Wagon, My Folks Claimed The Plains, My Folks And The One-Room Schoolhouse, My Folks' Depression Days* and the newest edition, *My Folks And The Civil War.* The opinions expressed are those of the people who lived through the War. We make no claim to complete historical accuracy; minimal updating of spelling, grammar and punctuation has been made to facilitate easier reading while maintaining the spirit and style of the authors.

World War II was a turning point in American history. We came together as a country to protect ourselves, defend our allies and ensure a peaceful future for generations to come. For those who are too young to remember, for those who can never forget; we proudly share this collection of memories with you.

Samantha Adams

CONTENTS

CHAPTER 1: An Overview Of The War Years

Respite On The Radio

The Selective Service was busy calling up draftees, and many more were enlisting. Of course my dad went right down to enlist. Unfortunately, he was 55 years old and had been gassed and shell-shocked in World War I. Never one to stand aside, he began to apply for jobs at defense plants and was hired on right away.

Other changes occurred on the home front. We were urged to conserve everything for the war effort. We saved grease. Every kid on the block had a tin-foil ball. Mine eventually got huge, because I begged every piece of tin foil from everyone I knew.

About this time our car was put up on blocks out in the yard, and my dad began riding with a neighbor to work. Tires were not for sale at any price. Enterprising individuals took advantage of the situation, and the black market was born. For enough money you could get anything you wanted. But, daddy said we didn't need anything that bad, so we managed on our ration books and little red and blue points.

We raised chickens, rabbits, ducks, geese and sometimes a hog. Daddy knew a beekeeper, and we traded chickens, eggs or what-ever he needed for some honey to help stretch our sugar. As far as I know, the bees were exempt from rationing.

Because we couldn't use our car and Daddy wasn't home much, the radio became my focus. I couldn't get enough of Jack

Armstrong, "Terry and the Pirates" and all the rest of the programs. Each had a War theme and fought spies and fascists tooth-and-nail. "Captain Midnight" became my favorite program. One bright spot emerged each week as we tuned into "Amos & Andy" and tried to forget the horror that was going on all over the world. Even the plot lines on the soap operas were about the War. "One Man's Family" had at least two of the sons in the service and mentioned some of the things we were all doing to help win the War.

It is so strange to think back about how patriotic we all were and how we didn't mind at all going without, because it was for the war effort.

And the War brought many surprises. One day a knock was heard at our door. I went to see who it was. There, standing with dufflebag in hand, was a young man. I called Momma, because I didn't know who it was. The young man said he was my cousin — Momma's nephew whom she had not seen since he was a baby. He was stationed at an Army camp in our town. After that he was a frequent visitor at our house, often bringing several buddies along for a home-cooked meal. It was a thrilling time for me, and I loved hearing all those young men talking and laughing. Sad to remember, many of those fine young men didn't return home.

Those war years were bad, and we were all glad when peace came at last.

Winnie Schuetz
Tilden, Illinois

Memories Catch The Spirit Of The Times

I was a little girl during World War II, and I remember my mother crying on Pearl Harbor Day. She said my brother, Earl, would have to go to War.

Earl enlisted in the U.S. Army infantry and had a Black Panther patch on his uniform. Mama would send him "Talelights" and other items from *Grit*. My Aunt Dorothy was an Army nurse and sent wonderful perfume from France.

Mama wrote Earl often. He said anything was interesting —

even when Susie, the barn cat, had another litter of kittens. We had a victory garden, and Mama canned a lot. My dad worked on a dairy farm.

When we could, we liked to go to the movies at Binghamton, New York. People would cheer when enemy planes were shot down in the newsreels. Also, there would be air-raid drills, and we were sent home from school. No lights could be shown during a blackout; an enemy bomber could see a lighted match at ground level. It was scary.

Kids collected milkweed insides for Navy fliers' vests.

One thing different then from now is that young and old, men and women could contribute to the war effort. There was this feeling that we were all in it together, and the United States was great.

Helen Williams
Millville, Pennsylvania

Red Cross Notifies Father Of New Son

Our family was hit hard in World War II. I felt so sorry for my poor mother, she had two sons and two in-laws in the service. Brother Alvin was a veterinarian in the Army Air Corps in Westover Field, Massachusetts, and he didn't leave the States.

Brother Bill had to leave college and join the Army, working with a supply division of the 902nd Air Engineering Squadron in Erding, Germany.

One day while he and his buddy were unloading ammunition from their truck, the truck was bombed. It was his buddy's turn in the truck while Bill was outside. His buddy was killed instantly, and Bill was hit, so his clothing caught fire. He rolled into a ditch. His sergeant figured they were both killed and didn't check until he heard Bill groan.

They found him unconscious and rushed him to the hospital. He was badly burned on his body, so the Army wrote home to my folks that he was "slightly injured." Today, at the age of 71, he still has health problems from this injury.

3

One son-in-law, Alfred Pollman, served in the Air Force at Westover Field, and he didn't leave the States. Another son-in-law, Walter Opfer, wasn't so lucky. He was in the Army in Germany with the 9th Armored Division in the final days of the War.

It so happened that his wife, Marybelle, was staying with my family in Norton, Kansas, while Walt was overseas. Their little son David was born on December 17. We hadn't heard from Walt for awhile, so I called the Red Cross to get word to him about his new son.

It took nearly two weeks, but finally the phone rang one Sunday noon, and they wanted to talk to Marybelle. We both were frightened about what we would hear, but it turned out to be a telegram from Germany from Walter saying, "Glad to hear we have a son. Hope you are both OK."

She hung up the telephone, and we both had a good cry just knowing he was OK.

Emilie A. Bird
Beatrice, Nebraska

Rumblings Of War

Thinking about World War II brings memories flooding back. The rumblings in Germany had long been disturbing my dad who was a World War I veteran. Many evenings we would sit by the table as he read the paper after supper. He would always say, "Mark my words, Germany wants power and there will be big trouble for all the world."

As one by one the little countries of Europe were overwhelmed, we studied them in school. I tried to picture the people in my mind and what it must be like to see their homes destroyed and their lives ruined. Then I would cry, and Momma would ask what was the matter. When I told her, she was sad, because she was an orphan, too.

On Saturday at the movies, I would watch the terrible news films and boo along with the other kids when we saw Hitler or

Mussolini. Dunkirk was a chance to cheer the rescue of thousands of men saved by the efforts of the Royal Navy. Assisted by hundreds of people of all ages — in boats of all sizes — the navy crossed and re-crossed the English Channel. Even today when I hear a broadcast of Churchill's "we shall fight" speech, I still get goose bumps.

Winnie Schuetz
Tilden, Illinois

Doing Without Was Not Bad At All

My brother was home on leave in the summer of 1941, a young, handsome 17- year- old.

Little did we know when we bid him goodbye as he left for the *USS Arizona* that we would never see him again. He was a gunner on ship and is now entombed under the *USS Arizona* Memorial.

We were a big family of 15. One by one, the brothers enlisted in the Navy, the Army and the Marines, until I had six more brothers in the service. All six of them came home after the War was over.

My brother in the Marines wrote home to our mother and said, "Wars are fought by Mothers like you at home, as much as us boys out here." I often wondered how my mother and father ever stood it. Having one boy killed, then six others leaving them — not knowing what would happen to them.

Mrs. James Gray
Rockton, Illinois

Plenty Of Shortages

When I met my wife, she was employed at a defense plant. I went to work making ship masts and pontoons for defense. I earned 60 cents an hour, time-and-a-half over 40 hours. I worked 10 hours a day, six days a week and some Sundays.

I finally saved enough money to buy a 1929 Studebaker, which

I pushed almost as far as I drove. Apartments were scarce and hard to get. The Office of Price Administration set the rent, but many landlords didn't follow guidelines. They also charged 50 cents a week each if you used over a 40-watt bulb, had a fan, had a radio or used their iron and board.

A lot of old houses were made into apartments. Usually the bath was shared by several apartments. Toilet paper was scarce, so you carried it to the bathroom and back to your apartment.

My wife and I were looking for an apartment once, walking the streets. The landlord had only to put out a for-rent sign, and it was taken that day. I was carrying our suitcase, which had our skillet, two pans, dishes, silver, a blanket and all our clothes, with room to spare.

After walking half a day with no luck, I left the suitcase in the bus station. My wife feared it would be stolen. I said, "let somebody steal it and get surprised." After walking another three hours, we saw a sign and rented two rooms, bath down the hall. Our suitcase was waiting for us.

You stood in line to get many things, including cigarettes. The lines would reach around the block.

My wife washed my dirty clothes in the shower with a scrub brush and hand soap. Laundry soap was unavailable. You could find no shorts for men, no sheets, hose, or ladies' panties with elastic. Clothespins were unavailable, so my wife hung our clothes on the line with the few big safety pins she had.

Hollis Kelsey
Henryetta, Oklahoma

Youth And Health Lost To War

My brother was in World War II and came back a different man from the healthy young man who left. He was wounded and sent home in a straitjacket. He's been 100 percent disabled ever since and in hospitals and nursing homes now for 25 years.

Pauline Longnecker
West Plains, Missouri

School Days And Sugar Rationing

During school vacation, I visited relatives near Chicago. I worked for Douglas Air Craft as a file clerk. I had never been in a large factory before. There was a huge pile of fine coal outside our department. This had to be moved around to prevent spontaneous combustion. Our department was a dirty mess. The employees were dirty from head to foot. My hair was light brown, but at night it was black.

Fabric was hard to find. One of the stores received a shipment. I bought my mother enough material for a housedress. We could rarely find sheer hose. I was surprised to find plenty of them in the Chicago area. I could only buy them in packages of three pairs. People who had charge accounts with mail-order companies could buy bedding, overalls and shirts most of the time. My cousin could buy overalls in Chicago all the time. He kept my dad and brother-in-law supplied.

Lois Finke Caldwell
Garnett, Kansas

Feed Sacks And Soldier Sons

Both of my sons were in World War II. We rationed many things; we couldn't even buy any kind of material to make dresses. We who raised little chickens and bought chicken food in 100-pound sacks used the food sacks to make our dresses and slips. The sacks came in many different colors with flowers, etc. We tried to buy two or three sacks of chicken food alike to use for a dress, or trade with a neighbor if they had or needed one the other had. But we were more concerned about the boys in the War.

My youngest son had his 18th birthday on the ship taking him to war, after he had been several months in training in the States. He had never spent a night away from home till he was inducted. Even when he had worked for a farmer all day, he walked two miles to the farm and back every day. They tried to get him to stay overnight, but he insisted on being home every night.

Our older son was injured in the service, the youngest was in the military police; he was gone three years. They are now grand-parents and have their own homes.

Ruth Jincks
Bethany, Missouri

A Lonesome Kind Of Life

I remember the World War II days very well. I was a teenager, and it was sad to see all the young men and women going off to War. There was not a young man left on the streets of Eldon, Missouri. The older men and women went to work in the stores and factories, and hundreds of women, girls and old men went to Kansas City to work in defense plants.

It was a different kind of life during World War II. It was a longing, sad, lonesome kind of life.

Sophie Wood
Eldon, Missouri

Scott Of The K-9 Corps

In 1943, Ernie Archer kept three portraits on the wall in his room. One was of his sister in a WAVE uniform, one was of his brother in a Coast Guard uniform and the third was of his dog, Scott.

Ten-year-old Ernie couldn't join the service. "And I didn't have any aluminum pots and pans to donate for the war effort," he recalls, "so I gave Scott to Dogs for Defense."

Scott was 18 months old then. He'd belonged to Ernie since he was a fluffy gold-and-white pup. Small for a collie, slight of build, Scott was lively and affectionate. He loved to play games with Ernie, especially the game of chase-around-and-under-the-dining-room-table. It wasn't easy for Ernie to part with Scott, but Dogs for Defense needed spunky, intelligent dogs.

Dogs for Defense contributed at least 20,000 dogs to the K-9 Corps. Dogs accepted for service had to be at least one year old, neither docile nor high-strung, and — above all — obedient and intelligent. The relationship between dog handler and dog was one of mutual trust and respect. When a handler was killed, his dog was destroyed because no one else could control his particular dog.

Dogs served in the Arctic, Europe and the South Pacific. The K-9s soon proved their worth, cave-scouting and investigating bamboo huts where the enemy might be hiding. They were especially useful on night duty after they learned to warn their handlers without barking. Dogs saved countless human lives, but many lost their own.

At the War's end, dogs were returned to the United States. In 1946, a notice came asking if the Archers wanted Scott back. They did. His picture still hangs in the Archer home beside his honorable discharge certificate, symbol of all the gallant dogs of the K-9 Corps.

Originally printed in *Capper's*.
By Jean Ciavonne
Colorado Springs, Colorado

CCC Work Makes Life Better For All

Our nation was just starting to recover from the Great Depression, and misery and need were everywhere. God sent us a great leader, a crippled, sickly man in a wheelchair. Many looked at his weakened body and could not see the indomitable spirit of the leader and his courageous wife. He gave us a plan to recover from the Depression: the Public Works Administration and the Civilian Conservation Corps.

The PWA went to work on the roads. Men found they could stand shoulder-to-shoulder and do the impossible. And glory be, they were paid to do it. You could ride by and hear them singing.

I was 17 when my younger brother and I joined the CCC. Not

every young man could join the CCC, only sons of low-income families that were without work. There were 10 of us children, and only my brother and I were allowed to go. We received $8 a month and room and board; $22 a month was sent to our mother to help the rest of the family.

I reported to Neodesha, Kansas. We were housed in barrack-type buildings with a mess hall and a doctor on duty. We arose to reveille, and lights out to taps.

This company was assigned to do conservation on area farms. All work was done by hand. We dug rocks from fields and pastures and transported them by wheelbarrows to the locations where they were needed. At the relocation site, we would beat them into size and shape with sledgehammers. Smaller rocks were crushed finer for lime to put back on the fields they were removed from, and larger ones for gravel on the roads. We dug cactuses from the fields and pastures and burned them.

When we built terraces, we became a shovel brigade, building them completely by hand.

When I was drafted in 1942, I realized how much I had learned in the CCC to make basic training, and Army life, easier for me.

> Jack Clifford
> As told to D. M. Clifford
> Garber, Oklahoma

Community Pulled Together

We lived in a farming community during the War. It seemed that all of us were busy in the war effort every day.

We children all had a container that we filled with nails we picked up. We also collected aluminum scraps. During school months we rolled bandages and made card table covers for use in USOs. Those mitered corners were something else!

The community had War Bond drives that included box socials, pie suppers and selling cakes. I remember cakes being auctioned for a sizeable sum, then turned back and sold again.

Then there was rationing. I remember taking a toothpaste tube in so another tube could be purchased, waiting until we could have a pair of shoes, collecting sugarless recipes, learning war songs and feeling proud.

There were posters everywhere. My favorite was the one with an American flag and a bomber. The words "Keep 'em flying," were printed on it. That one is still portrayed on the side of a huge brick building in a local town.

Glenna Turner
Hardesty, Oklahoma

Premonition Of War

Many who farmed during the Depression days of the 1930s — who survived drought, grasshoppers and dust storms — started looking for better-paying jobs. My husband and I were among them. My husband got a job with an aircraft company in Wichita, Kansas, and commuted to work from our hometown of Winfield. It seemed like half the town did the same, men and women alike.

Then came Pearl Harbor Day. We had gone for a pleasure drive through the countryside, coming home to learn of the terrible disaster. We couldn't believe it. It quickly became a reality, with rationing and shortages of all kinds.

I learned to make soap from all the grease I could save up — soap was almost nonexistent in stores. Many used coffee grounds twice, or added a little fresh grounds to yesterday's in the percolator. Honey and molasses were used instead of sugar.

Linoleum was practically non-existent, too. When the day came I could buy a new linoleum rug, I was so happy! We had a battery radio, and when the news came on, we were glued to it. The daily newspaper put out "extras" to keep people informed.

After the War had gone on long enough for German prisoners to be sent to the United States, I was driving by a friend's house in the country and saw this prisoner in prison garb walking along the road. I notified the sheriff, but the man had vanished. I later learned he had stopped at my friend's house and got a drink from the well. Their dog barked. The man was very frightened and spoke to the dog in a foreign language, then left in a hurry. My friend didn't go out, but watched him. He was probably starved, having run away from the prison camp. War is terrible for everyone.

I am now 80 years old, but I still remember those terrible years. I have felt since that perhaps the aircraft factories had a premonition of things to come, as my husband started working 12 hours a day a long time before Pearl Harbor. For peace time I thought that was strange.

Mrs. Clay W. Archer
Iola, Kansas

Navy Man's Code

When I was six, my dad enlisted in the U. S. Navy and trained at Great Lakes Naval Training Station. After boot camp, he came home briefly, then went back to await further assignment in the Outgoing Unit near Chicago. When he received his orders, he called to tell us that he would be sent to Key West, Florida, for training in sonar.

Fearing she would not be able to see him for quite a while, my mother asked him if she should come to Chicago. Of course, he said yes, and they decided then and there to meet at the railway station the coming Friday. Little did they think that so simple a direction could turn into such a nightmare.

Being from a small town in Iowa, they did not count on Chicago having more than one railway station. Dad was waiting at one, while Mother, who had ridden the midnight train arriving about dawn, was waiting at the other. As the morning wore on, it was obvious that their simple directions were useless and that something must be done or they would never meet.

Unaccustomed to the bustle of the big city, Mother could do no more than wait while Dad frantically tried to find her.

About noon, he decided to go to the other station, but by this time Mother had taken a taxi to the Drake Hotel, where she sat in the lobby almost in tears.

It was then that the kind lady volunteer at the Travelers Aid Society desk noticed Dad, who was pacing back and forth nearby.

"Can I help you?" she asked. "Are you expecting to meet someone?"

"Yes, I'm supposed to meet my wife here at 7:30 a.m., and she didn't show up. I sure would appreciate it if you could help me find her."

After finding that Mother's train had been on time, the lady got in touch with her colleague at the other station. Yes, there had been a young lady waiting, and no, she was not there anymore. In little more than an hour, the desk at the Drake Hotel called to say that they believed that the tearful lady waiting there in the lobby was the missing person. That was all Dad needed; he took a taxi to the Drake post haste.

That meeting was a historic one. Mother, who liked big hats, was wearing one the size of a satellite dish. When she spied Dad coming across the lobby, she threw caution to the wind. As the picture hat went cartwheeling down the marble steps, she fell into his arms, and all problems seemed to be at an end.

But all the hotels were full up. Again, Travelers Aid came to the rescue. They wheedled the Hilton people into letting a poor Seaman 1st Class get a room with his wife before shipping out. Then the incident we later called "the code story" came to pass.

Tired from her strenuous journey, and relieved by a clean bed, Mother promptly fell asleep while Dad talked. He had devised an elaborate "code," which he said he would include in his letters to help her know where he was at the moment. Knowing his letters would be censored, he had a plan that he felt was foolproof. But Mother was sound asleep and to this day cannot tell you what the plan, so cleverly devised, was. He thought all through the War that they knew where he was, while in fact they had no idea.

My memories of the War were grim. I was just old enough to overhear their late-night conversations and to worry where my daddy might be. In 1945, Dad came home for Christmas and found to his surprise that we had no idea where he had been (he was on a Navy tug in the South Pacific).

Now we often joke about the "code" and wonder if it would have really worked if Mother had not fallen asleep.

Harriet Wolford
Grand Junction, Colorado

First Woman On Job

At one job I had during World War II, I was the first female employee in the plant. When I walked in the door the first day, all the men in the place had assembled to see "what she looks like." The man who introduced me to the first punch press I ever saw said, "You will do well to do 1,500 parts an hour."

The first day I did 700 an hour. The second day, I did 900 an hour. Third day, 1,100 an hour. Then I hit it. I was doing 3,000 an hour and loving it, when I glanced up to find myself surrounded by men. One man said, "You go and sit in the washroom for a while. You are making it look bad for us." I went. I was scared.

Not long after that I was transferred to another job operating a crane that picked up stacks of metal landing mats. I dipped them in a vat of acid and then in a vat of rinse solution, and from there set them on skids. It moved across the area on an overhead trolley and was operated by an instrument held in the hand, with push buttons to control the movement. I became so proficient at operating it that my supervisor said, "You set them down on a dime." One day I looked up to see the production manager watching me with a look of awe on his face. Guess they thought only men could operate things like that. Later they hired a number of other women. They had learned that women were capable of something besides washing dishes and having babies.

Mary Gardener
Forest Park, Illinois

A Moment's Thought

Somewhere on an island
In outreaches of Pacific's blue,
Some soldier is giving his life
For peace; forever pure and true.

He's dying for the cause of freedom
And the American way of life.
May his sacrifice ne'er be forgotten
For he died in the midst of strife.

Ah, you say you didn't know him
He wasn't your relative or friend.
Perhaps he wasn't, but someone
Is proud he fought bravely to the end.

He's the son of some dear parents
And for him their hearts do bleed,
Because he went down like a soldier
Fighting those sons of Satan's greed.

You who have sons or brothers
Or sweetheart far away,
Stop and think just an instant —
Are they ALL coming back someday?

I was in high school when this poem was written in 1944.
                              Nova Felkins Bailey
                              Beaverton, Oregon

Seven Sons In the War

This is about my husband's parents, Mr. and Mrs. Ray Herdman. Six of their sons were in the Army, and one in the Navy. No family in America had more sons serve their country in that War.

My in-laws lived on a farm in Piper, Kansas. Service flags were very popular then and hung in the windows of homes, with a star for each son in the service. None were available with seven stars, but a special one was made in Valley Forge, Pennsylvania.

My in-laws were very lucky, as all seven sons returned home safe and sound. I was also lucky to meet one son, Eugene, who was stationed at Fort Mead, Maryland, my home state at the time.

We have been married for 46 years and have a son who has served his country with the Navy for 16 years.

Roberta Herdman
Kansas City, Kansas

Sad News

The knocking on the kitchen door was persistent that Saturday morning in June 1945. The door opened and there stood a very somber-faced man. "Is your father home?" he asked.

"Yes, he's in the living room," I answered, and pointed him in that direction.

Crossing the dining room he could see Dad sitting in a rocker reading a paper. As Mr. Anderson reached the door of the living room he said, "Frank, I have some sad news for you."

Dad jumped up and blurted out, "Them damn Japs!"

By this time I was at the living room door.

Mr. Anderson was perplexed by Dad's outburst and asked, "Have you gotten word already?"

"No. This is the first. But there are times when I can sense that a loved one is in trouble even though the person may be far away."

The sad news brought that day by Mr. Anderson, Red Cross contact person for our county, was that Verlis, one of my brothers, had been killed in action in the Philippines on May 26. With Troop C, 7th Cavalry, of the First Cavalry Division, he had fought in numerous battles from New Guinea to the Philippines. We would later learn that he died near the town of Infanta on Luzon as he led his squadron up a hill.

Breaking into tears I returned to the kitchen. My younger sisters asked why I was crying. I said, " We have lost Verlis." One immediately wanted to go tell Mother who was supervising a chicken house chore.

"No. You stay here. I'll go tell her."

Being a naive teenager, it never occurred to me that Dad should be the one to break the sad news to Mother.

As I neared the chicken house Mother saw that I was upset and asked, "Nova, what is the matter?"

"Verlis was killed."

Hearing those words Mother went to pieces. At no other time did I ever see her so upset.

By now Dad and Mr. Anderson had come outside. Dad took Mother by the hand, and with his arm around her shoulder led her back indoors.

Shortly Mr. Anderson left.

As word spread through our rural county, friends and neighbors called to offer condolences. Some had suffered similar losses.

Some days later we sisters were discussing our loss with Mother. She told us that several days previously, she didn't remember just how long, on awakening one morning Dad had told her: "One of the boys was in a really tight spot last night." We concluded that it was near the time of Verlis' death.

Brother Jim, in the Army Air Force in England, had awakened one night weeping. He, too, sensed that Verlis was badly hurt. Verlis was two years his senior.

Eventually Verlis' personal effects were received at home — a small box containing his wallet, a watch and a few family pictures. Later his medals — a Bronze Star, a Silver Star, and two Purple Hearts — also arrived.

My parents took the option to have Verlis' remains returned to native soil. They were reinterred in the soldier's section of Collinsville Cemetery in Collinsville, Oklahoma.

Nova Felkins Bailey
Beaverton, Oregon

No Grand Adventure

As for World War II, I should be able to give you some sort of high adventure story. Such is not the case. There was a popular saying that it took eight men to be behind the man behind the gun. I was one of those eight in a supporting role as an aviation metalsmith in the U.S. Navy Reserve. The only enemy action I saw was a fistfight in the Pearl Harbor Ford Island Air Station beer hall!

My job in the metal shop was much like the work I had been doing at Lockheed Aircraft, except for the management and training methods. Our work was pretty routine, with much boredom and waiting for something to happen. I think that this may well have been our last popular war. All the civilian population was supportive, saving empty aluminum toothpaste tubes and worn-out aluminum cookware as well as discarded kitchen grease as contributions to the war effort. People actually looked for an out-of-town soldier boy or sailor to take home for Sunday dinner.

Rex O. Wonnell
San Jose, California

What I Didn't Expect In The Navy

When we were thrown into an unexpected war by the bombing of Pearl Harbor on December 7, 1941, I knew almost immediately that I would be inducted into one of the branches of the military, probably the Army. I had always leaned toward the Navy as one branch of the service that I would like, so I enlisted for the term of four years as a reservist, and in January of 1942 reported for active duty at the age of 25.

I was immediately given the rate of Yeoman 3rd class, the reason being that I was qualified for office work, although I had very little office experience. I detested the confinement of office work. I am an outdoor person.

I was disappointed that I wasn't given a rating as motor machinist mate or something of that caliber. However, I discovered the reason for the yeoman rating. I was a fast typist — 85 to 90 words a minute — and capable of 150 words a minute in shorthand. I found myself in one of the most interesting of occupations, court martial reporting. My advancement up the ranks to chief yeoman was very fast, taking less than two years.

Working as a court reporter at the Naval Air Station, Trinidad, British West Indies, was fascinating. I also worked with the judge advocate preparing cases, such as researching, drawing up charges and specifications, etc. As a court reporter, I was required to take all the testimony in shorthand and transcribe it that evening so it could be read back at the start of court the next day. Many a night I worked until midnight.

As a court-martial reporter in the Navy I was privy to most every type of crime, ranging from AWOL to desertion, embezzlement of ships service funds, murder, dereliction of duty, sleeping on watch and of course many minor incidents. After my four-year enlistment I had no desire to make a career of court reporting, mostly because I would have had to learn machine shorthand. I also found court reporting to be rather stressful.

Francis E. Hager
Sun City, Arizona

From Cannery To Marine Duty

My mother, Ellen Miller (Albany, Oregon), wrote to me about the effects of World War II on our family. She said, "On the day World War II started we were living in a tiny apartment in Yakima, Washington. Donnie was just two months old, and Dad was working at a cannery warehouse. I remember the next day, people were out frantically buying anything that might be rationed eventually.

Sometime in the spring of 1942, Dad went to work for E.I. Dupont out of Hanford, Washington. We had no idea what they were planning. It was all very hush-hush. Dad's job was driving an Army stretch-out bus transporting high-level officials from meeting to meeting in Washington and Oregon. After that job ended, Dad was working again in the cannery. After Jerry was born in

1943, Dad went to work at the Hanford works as a carpenter.

Dad was always told he couldn't volunteer for the service because he was a Canadian citizen, but in June of 1944 he was drafted and signed up for the Marines. He left Yakima on Friday, June 24. His mother was very ill at the time. When it was discovered his mother was near death, the Marines sent Dad back — he had gotten as far as Seattle. He arrived home to see his mother on Monday morning before she passed away.

The boys in the service all came home for the funeral — Dick, his older brother, came from the Canadian Army; Doug from the Navy Seabees; Lee from the American Army; and of course, Dad.

After the funeral all the boys went back to their various bases. Dad's next trip home was in September for boot camp leave.

It was a busy time with three little ones, and it was not easy on the tiny allotment check we received, but we survived, and all the boys from our family came home safely. (In spite of the fact that Dad was in the first wave of Marines to reach Japan.)

Dad was discharged from the Marines in December 1945. We all went back to "normal" living, still with shortages, especially housing and jobs.

Jerry Miller
Huffman, Texas

The Last Goodbye

One of the saddest memories for me happened on October 19, 1942, when my brother Arnold had to leave for the Army. We took him to Grundy Center, Iowa, to be inducted. From there he went by train to Iowa Falls, Iowa, and then on to Fort Hood, Texas. This train we called Toonerville always came right behind our house. That morning at 3:30 a.m. the train came by, very soon after we had returned home from Grundy Center. This time Arnold was on the train. He stood on the platform on the back of the train, and as it passed by our house, Arnold called out over and over, "Bye, Pa and Mom!"

The goodbye of that early morning hour was long in my mother's memory. Arnold was never to return home. On July 22, 1943, Arnold lost his life in a tank at the Invasion of Sicily.

Leonard Gelder
Wellsburg, Iowa

A Tearful Farewell

Pearl Harbor Day shares its place, to me, with the day my younger brother John left to begin his service in the Army. I can hear him yet, hurrying down the stairs after one final farewell look around his bedroom. I stood in the bathroom, crying for him and for us, as he came through for a quick kiss and hug before going on out to bid his mother goodbye. She was braver than me. She didn't cry until after he was gone.

I'm sure I would have cried even harder had I known we wouldn't get to see him again for more than three years. I knew many men and boys in the service, but never knew of any except John who didn't get his leave until after finishing basic training.

He was trained to set up and run a switchboard in the field. He was needed to accompany some particular unit, but this one thing has always seemed terribly unfair to me.

The present mobile generation — used to speeding autos, flights, and viewing on TV places they have never been — can have no idea of the trauma experienced by boys who had never even been to high school or farther than 50 miles from home when they were suddenly forced to leave home and loved ones. Some did fine. Others had to be weeded out, and still others did their own weeding. For example, one shy boy I met while teaching school *accidentally* shot himself in the foot while hunting the day before he was to be inducted.

The wife of an old friend of our family felt she had to see her husband one more time before he was shipped out. This young mother, after leaving her baby in the nursery, stood in line for a ticket knowing there weren't enough available for all who were in line. Just as she was almost at the front, with a ticket a sure thing, her name was called over the loudspeaker with orders from the nursery to come at once. She burst into tears as she saw any chance for a ticket going down the drain, but the sympathy and camaraderie of the time took over, and those next in line to her promised to hold her place until she could get back.

I'm sure the trip itself was crowded and difficult. And what did she gain by it? Just the opportunity to stand with the crowd as her husband marched by with his squadron. He did come back to spend many happy years with her, but I'm sure many other wives saw one last glimpse of their husbands under similar circumstances.

I had made a bargain with my brother that I would teach our home school as long as he was gone. My first term began two or three days after he left, and I was in my fourth term when he returned after nearly three and one-half years.

During that time he had circled the earth by train and ship, touching all continents except South America and Antarctica. Our nomad was happy to be alive and to cease his wanderings.

Marjorie Crouch
Uvalde, Texas

Over The Hill

I was a young farm boy in 1942 and wanted to serve my country. My dad took me to the Salina, Kansas, Army Recruiting Station to enlist in the Army Air Corps. A great number of young men were enlisting and being drafted. I took the physical and was told to return home and they would notify me when I was needed.

I received my notice to report at Fort Riley, Kansas, on September 26th. I hitchhiked there, arriving on the 25th, and was assigned a bed in the barracks. I thought I would be inducted in a day or two. The second evening a sergeant called my name and told me to report for KP at 3 the next morning. I told him I hadn't been sworn in yet. He said since I was still a civilian I wouldn't be required to pull KP. Then the same thing happened daily until October 1st.

By that time, I was getting discouraged and decided the Army didn't need me. I asked for and received a pass to go into Junction City. I didn't stop there but hitchhiked to Wichita, where my brother-in-law and sister lived. When I explained that the Army didn't need me they said I was over the hill and was a deserter. I said I wasn't over the hill as I was still a civilian, and I didn't believe the Army needed me.

My sister was frantic and was sure the Army would have me shot. I finally agreed to return to Fort Riley on October 4th. The first night I was back the sergeant came after me. Before he could say anything I asked him where he had been, because I had missed him. He told me he had been looking for me. Again he told me to report for KP, and I explained I hadn't been sworn in. He came after me for KP each evening until October 10th. I had decided if they didn't swear me in that day I was leaving again and not returning. At 4 p.m. I was lined up with ten men outside the barracks and sworn in. The sergeant found me again that evening and assigned me to KP. Right after he left I was called to the office and given an envelope with my records and told I would ship out the next morning. When I found the sergeant and told him I was leaving, I thought he would cry.

I may have the record for being the only one to go over the hill before I was inducted.

Ivan French
Mercedes, Texas

Roses Among The Thorns

The bombing of Pearl Harbor on December 7, 1941, shocked the whole nation. My husband and I were visiting some very dear friends when the program on the radio was interrupted, and the news announced that Pearl Harbor had been bombed. We sat in stunned silence. Our hearts were saddened. There was a terrible feeling of uneasiness. We knew our lives would never be the same.

All afternoon and evening the news worsened. We did not leave the radio for anything as they told of the sinking of the *USS Arizona* and the hundreds of lives lost.

A draft of men 18 years of age and up had already been set up, and it sounded as though all able-bodied men would be called into the service. My husband was soon drafted and went into the service January 14, 1943. I managed to tell him goodbye without shedding a tear, but after he boarded the bus and was out of sight, a regular torrent evolved.

The bus that day carried my husband to Fort Leavenworth, Kansas. While he was at Leavenworth waiting for assignment, his mother, father and I went to see him.

When he came out to meet us, his expression was one of anger and displeasure. I couldn't figure out what was wrong. When he finally told me, I laughed out loud. He was angry because we had seen him as he was. The baggy Army fatigues, the Army haircut, the heavy boots and general appearance was not the well-groomed person I was used to seeing, but what the heck! I would have been glad to see him in anything, as long as I could see him. We had a good visit before he was shipped out to Virginia.

From Virginia, he was sent to Clearwater, Florida, for basic training. He trained on the ocean-front beaches, slept in one of the hotels that had been taken over to house Army personnel, basked in the sun, and except for the longing to be home, actually enjoyed the time.

During the time he was in basic training there, my birthday came around. I was pleasantly surprised when I received a dozen red roses from the florist that day. I knew he didn't have much money and had probably spent most of what he had on me. That really touched me. It didn't touch me as much as the phone call I received that evening asking for me to send him some money. He had spent every penny he had to send me those roses.

Although the heartache, separation and financial burden of caring for a young child was the same for thousands of other servicemen's wives, I seem — after all these years — to recall some of the lighter things that happened with regard to our family .

Other little things happened that we could laugh about — something that we couldn't do very often. Those were very sad days, and a little joy was a welcome emotion.

Zoe Rexroad
Adrian, Missouri

While You're Away

While you're on some foreign shore
Fighting for those you love,
I'll think of you each passing day
And pray each night to God above,
To protect and guide you right,
While you're away.

I'll dream of you and days we knew,
Those days so precious to just us two,
While you're there I'll do my share
To win this war and lasting peace
So happiness may never cease.

While you're away often I'll write
To bring you cheer while in the fight,
To give courage and hope anew.
I'll be true and wait for you
While you're away.

I was in high school when this poem was written in 1945.

Nova Felkins Bailey
Beaverton, Oregon

You Are Not Supposed To Be Here

Gasoline and tires were rationed during World War II. We seldom used the car except for my husband, an Army officer, who drove to work six days a week at the newly opened Camp Detrick in Frederick, Maryland.

One Sunday afternoon we decided we would take our small baby and drive around. We were from the south, and wanted to see the beautiful Maryland country with its apple and cherry orchards.

We found a wooded mountain road and drove up it. It ended in a clearing, with some buildings in the woods beyond. Two men stopped our car.

"You are not supposed to be here," one said. "Turn around and go back. This is private property." We apologized and left.

An item in the paper caught my attention the next week. It stated that President Franklin Roosevelt had spent the weekend relaxing at his secret Shangri-la retreat in the Catoctin Mountains.

We had driven into Shangri-la, which is still used by the presidents, but is now called Camp David.

Gypsy Damaris Boston
Shreveport, Louisiana

No Age Limit On Patriotism

There were days when I fingered that little bit of change jingling in my coat pocket and thought of other ways I'd like to "invest" it. But those thoughts never lasted long when I saw kids generously forfeit their milk or candy money to help our fighting men and women.

Even today, though I can't remember his name, I can still hear the bond chairman shouting: "If you can't shoulder a gun, shoulder the cost of one." I can remember the flocks of men and women eagerly buying their War Bonds. They were people with hope, with faith in God and country. It taught me a lifelong lesson: that there is power and beauty in the act of working together for a common cause. And there is no age limit on patriotism!

J. P. Holden
Vancouver, Washington

Town Pulls Together

Our small, quiet village of White Pigeon, Michigan, was a hub of activity in the daytime during World War II. My grandmother Reed, a widowed lady, owned and operated Reed's Book Store downtown on U.S. 112, the main route between Detroit and Chicago. A soda fountain in the rear of the brick structure attracted residents to create conversation each morning and share their latest news about men and women away in the armed services.

When word reached our close-knit townspeople that young Frank Cerny was missing in action, everyone was saddened. I was a scared teenager thinking about my two brothers and brother-in-law serving overseas. What if this happened to our family?

I shuddered to think of the possibility. My oldest brother, Robert Reed, and Frank were in the 1940 graduating class from the local high school. Soon after finishing school they were inducted into the service with many other young men from our county. The evening the men boarded the bus in front of the courthouse at Centreville, families bid them goodbye. I stood with my family waving as the bus slowly pulled away from the curb, tears streaming down my face.

Then my other brother Richard graduated in 1941, and we stood at the farewell ceremony again, feeling fear as the bus departed for the second time in one year. It was almost more than Grandma could bear to see another grandson go to war.

Prayer vigils were held for the men and women serving in the armed forces. It brought the community together to hold rallies and parades to keep spirits high and urge letter writing to keep in touch. A steady stream of customers entered the store every day for the daily newspapers from points in Michigan and Indiana. People took time to sit at the soda fountain, scan the paper and share news that concentrated on their individual relatives.

On Saturday evenings families came to town from the rural areas. It was comforting to have letters read by mothers, grandmothers, sisters and brothers telling about life away in distant lands, some amusing, some sad.

Another shock came when my brother-in-law was taken into the Air Force. My sister also said farewell when she joined Jack in California. It was almost more than Grandma could bear. After the store closed, Grandma sat at the roll-top desk with a dim light, writing a message to each one absent from our family.

My friend and neighbor, Vesta Stickle, graduated in 1944. The future looked uncertain, so she enlisted to become an Army nurse. The people in the community were sensitive, and tears flowed when two more missing in action names were displayed in the park. I'll never forget those war years and the courage the home-town citizens displayed to strengthen the families of the men who gave the ultimate sacrifice for their country.

When the War ended, it was a celebration I'll always remember. When people were not in the store we stepped outside to join the street activity. It was difficult for the families who wouldn't be rejoined by their loved ones who served.

Phyllis M. Peters
Three Rivers, Michigan

World War II To A Teenager

I was 14 years old when Japan bombed Pearl Harbor. I was learning to put a crease in a pair of men's pants when I heard the news. Everyone was dumfounded! How could anyone dare attack us?

As if on cue, the people of our country banded together, rolled up our sleeves and prepared to defend what was ours. No loyal American neglected his or her part in defending our land, homes and families.

My family suffered through the shortages, sacrifices, rationing, air-raid warnings and the trauma of war as much as everyone else.

We suffered the loss of one of our own. Two of my brothers joined the fray in the spring of 1942. Tim joined the Naval Air Corps. His plane crashed on Puget Sound in October 1942. He and one other man survived the crash. Ray joined the Army Air Corps.

He didn't come back. His plane exploded in mid-air over New Guinea in the summer of 1944. He had received one letter telling about the birth of his daughter, Linda.

There are many firsts attributed to World War II. For the first time in history, women entered the armed services.

Women also went to work in shipyards, airplane factories and other war-related positions.

It was during World War II that women began shaving their legs. We were unaware of nylon. Ladies' hosiery was made of silk. But silk was being used for the war effort. No self-righteous lady would consider wearing the heavy, baggy, cotton stockings that were available. The answer was to go bare-legged.

My mother smoked cigarettes. They were not rationed, but they were not as readily available as they might have been. When the van came to our small town, Dallas, Oregon, delivering cigarettes to the stores, there was always a line of people waiting to buy some. The driver would sell each person two or three packs before he made his regular delivery. People purchased and smoked whatever they could get. All of the well-known brands of cigarettes were going overseas.

There were several farms between Dallas and Independence that had been owned by Japanese people who had been sent to internment camps. When we could find an unsuspecting person, we would ask, "and do you know what the authorities found in that barn after they were gone?" Curiously, they would answer, "No, what?" We would say, "Manure."

The government kept saying that the continental United States had never been shelled by enemy fire. Obviously, they did not want us to panic, and they did not want the Japanese to know how accurate they were. After the War, we learned our Pacific coastline had been hit by enemy fire in two different locations. An unexploded bomb — fired off the coast into the southern part of Oregon — was found by some children who were on a picnic with their pastor. Five of the children were killed when the bomb exploded.

Mr. Voth, a man of German descent, lived in the foothills of the Coastal Mountains range high above Dallas. He owned a dairy and a herd of cattle. At night, we often saw a searchlight cutting into the dark sky, originating from the direction of Mr. Voth's land. We wondered why a light of that magnitude was allowed to continue shining. After the War, we learned Mr. Voth was a German sympathizer signaling the enemy in code with the light. He was quietly sent to prison for his deeds.

When I was old enough to get a work permit, I started working in the Blue Lake Cannery in West Salem, Oregon. After the perishables such as corn, beans, carrots, etc. were canned, we dehydrated potatoes. One evening, the supervisor came to our area and announced, "Do an especially good job tonight, girls, because these are going to our boys." Surprised, I asked her where they had been going. She answered, "To Russia."

When the War was over, I was 18 years old, practically an old maid. I didn't really know how to date. My future husband was the older brother of my chums Violet and Virginia. Bob had been overseas for the duration of the War. We were married shortly after he came home.

Mary L. Hodson
Cornelius, Oregon

A War Department Message

The War in Europe seemed to be drawing to a close. Everyone had an ear glued to the news to hear the latest developments. News from our GI was sparse all the time he was overseas. The children haunted the mail box, only to be disappointed.

On March 19, my little son came to my bedroom with fear written all over his face. "Mommy, the depot agent is at the door, and he has a yellow envelope in his hand."

I put on my housecoat and opened the door. The yard was filled with all the neighbors, waiting to comfort us. The agent handed me the envelope and said. "It's a War Department message. I am very sorry." Everyone who saw him come to my house assumed that it was a death message.

Numbly I opened the telegram. It read, "Your husband has been declared missing in action."

The neighbors were so kind and helpful. Friends came and went all day offering to help us. In the evening, the legion commander and a friend came to see us. "We'd like to plan a memorial service for your husband," they said. I explained what the message had conveyed and how uncertain the outcome might be.

The following morning I made contact with the Red Cross, which was most willing to help, but they had received no messages to confirm what had happened. They contacted the National Red Cross, and it, too, was without any information.

One day the depot agent came again to deliver another message. The agent said, "At least it is not a death message."

The message read,"Your husband was returned to military control on April 26th." No details were made known.

The following Saturday a man who worked at the post office noticed a letter go through the line with an APO address. It was for me, and he knew there was no delivery on Saturday, so he brought it to the house.

It was from our GI. He said they had been captured by the Germans and since the War was nearly over, they were not supposed to take any prisoners and could not confine the Americans to prison camps. They marched these prisoners for 44 days, trying to find a place to put them. Every camp they approached, a runner came out and told them to go elsewhere. The only food they had to eat was potatoes left in the fields behind the diggers. These they boiled in their helmets. Sometimes they found some cabbage roots. Their health suffered a lot.

On June 1st he walked into my kitchen. In his hand he carried a dozen farm-fresh eggs. He couldn't tolerate potatoes, but he was hungry for eggs.

It was a happy reunion, but I could see how much he had changed. He was nervous, irritable and unable to tolerate crowds.

Madonna Storla
Postville, Iowa

31

Neighbor To The Rescue

It was a beautiful September day. Indian summer was really putting on a show, the year was 1939.

I was busy doing my housework, singing along with the radio, which was about the only means of communication with the outside world. The children were busy playing outside while my husband was out back repairing a sagging-down shed.

Suddenly the music stopped. An excitable voice on the radio said, "Attention folks, President Roosevelt has just declared war!"

I was stunned. Was I hearing right? I listened a minute longer then I ran out to tell my husband. The neighbor was already there, he too had heard. Soon there was a group of people in our yard discussing the announcement. Everyone was stunned. America at war again. The terrible World War I was over in 1918. It was supposed to be a war to end all wars.

Soon our boys were being drafted. It was a sad time for all, never knowing if they would return or not.

More supplies were needed — food for our boys overseas. They deserved the best; they were giving their best for our country.

Then came rationing. Once every month — and sometimes every two weeks — we received a book of blue ration stamps, sometimes they were of different hues but they were still the same.

We as a nation griped as always and many exchanged stamps. Substitutes for different foods were tried, and if you didn't have enough until your next book of stamps came out, you went without. People learned to be more conservative.

It seemed, though, there was always someone there in case of emergency to help out.

My baby boy Ernie was born in 1942. He was having problems digesting his milk. He seemed to be allergic to all milk formulas. Finally the doctor said to try Eagle Brand. It agreed with him and I thought the problem was over.

In those days, the only place you could buy Eagle Brand was in the drug store. It soon became hard to get as more people started using it to supplement their milk supply.

My doctor wrote a prescription for me, so I got some to help out, but I wasn't getting enough. The drug stores weren't getting as much Eagle Brand, so I was giving the baby a feeding of Eagle Brand one time and formula the next. I was beside myself. I hoped that Ernie would outgrow his problem.

Mr. McCall, who lived up the road a mile, stopped by one day with a quart of whole milk. "Do you think little Ernie can have this?" he asked.

For the first time in weeks, Ernie kept the milk down and slept so soundly all night that I got up several times to check on him.

After that, Mr. McCall supplied us with whole cow's milk until Ernie was weaned. He was an angel in disguise.

I think that when rationing was over and the boys came home was one of the most wonderful days of my life.

Evelyn Williams-Hall
Sioux City, Iowa

Family Members Are Drafted

It wasn't long before members of my family became part of the draft. One cousin was drafted July 16, 1941, as one of those who was to be gone only a year. He served 52 months in the Pacific area. My oldest brother, age 33, and a cousin left July 20, 1942. My brother was only in about 18 months. He had health problems and was given a medical discharge.

Men who were farmers were exempt, as food was a necessity. My mother was a widow and was allowed to keep one son to farm. After my oldest brother got a discharge, my youngest brother was drafted. He had not been old enough in 1942. He left February 19, 1944, on a train for Camp Fanin, Tyler, Texas. En route he contract-ed pneumonia, so he started his training in the hospital. This delayed his start in basic training, which may have been a blessing in disguise. The group he should have started with were all in the Battle of the Bulge, where many lives were lost.

As soon as his basic training was over, they were sent to Camp Mead, Maryland, and were loaded on a South American boat for their trip overseas. The trip was long, the food was bad and most everyone was seasick. Going through the Mediterranean Sea, they had a bad storm. Every two hours they had to change guard. They were strapped to the mast because the storm was so severe that they could not stand. The rains fell on them from above, and the waves washed over them from below. It was impossible to do any guarding. He wondered,"Why am I here?" They landed in Naples, Italy, and the storms still continued. There was a flood there and my brother lost all his personal things, even his watch.

They were on the front lines in Italy for 45 days and nights without relief. When they reached Austria, they met up with three other divisions, and the war was over. It was said to be the longest time any troops were on continuous duty.

Esther Carolus
Clarion, Iowa

———■———

CHAPTER 2: Pearl Harbor Remembered

In The Center Of History

On the morning of December 7, 1941, I was standing on the deck of the battleship *USS Tennessee* at Pearl Harbor. It seemed to be the beginning of another beautiful day, as were most of the days in the territory of Hawaii. The time was around 7:50 a.m., and I was pondering what I would do that day.

The mighty battleship *USS Arizona* was tied up just a few yards behind the *Tennessee*. I saw no one on the *Arizona* at that early hour, but the complete ship was not visible from my view because the superstructure of the *Tennessee* obstructed my view.

The battleship *USS West Virginia* was tied up along my ship and few men were out on the deck at that early hour. The *USS Maryland* was a few yards directly in front of my ship. The *USS Oklahoma*, which in a few minutes would be completely over-turned, was tied up next to the *Maryland*.

I had graduated from high school in 1938. Even though the Great Depression was over, jobs were not too numerous in the small mining-farming community where I lived. My brother joined the Navy around September 1939 and was sent to San Diego Naval Training Center for basic training. It seemed to me to be a wonderful way to see the world, so three months later I joined. To my dismay and disappointment I was sent to the Great Lakes training station, but it was still the farthest I had ever been from home. I never realized I would soon be in the center of the most remembered event of the 20th century.

As I stood on the deck that morning, I thought of my family back in Illinois and of Christmas Day not too far in the future. Suddenly planes began flying alongside battleship row. They were very low and very close to the ships. I could see the pilots very clearly. I stood and stared at them, and they in turn stared at me. One plane after another. One of the Japanese pilots waved to me, and I waved back. I do not recall how many planes there were in the group, but there were several.

I had written to my mother a few months before stating the Japanese would attack Pearl Harbor, but when the day came I did not realize that it could be happening. I only wondered: Why so many planes on a Sunday morning?

I could plainly see they were of Asiatic origin, yet still I could not believe they were Japanese and were there to attack. Suddenly I saw smoke, dirt and debris fly hundreds of feet in the air, and I heard a thunderous explosion. It was then I realized they were indeed Japanese and we were at war.

The rest is history. More than 2,400 servicemen gave their lives at a place that many Americans at that time did not know even existed. Hundreds of others, including myself, were injured.

If we are to be strong in the future we must remember the past. Remember Pearl Harbor — keep America alert.

Jack Doyle
Taylorville, Illinois

Tour Of The *USS Arizona*

In the fall of the year, on display in the harbor area of Los Angeles, California, was the latest built Navy ship, the *USS Arizona.*

Also on display was *Old Ironsides*, a wooden, handcrafted battleship built during the early settling of America. The public was allowed on both ships.

The crowd was large, and the line moved slow, but when on

board *Old Ironsides* you could rub your hand on the smooth wood and wonder how, with the limited tools of early America, such a sturdy, beautiful ship could be built.

Next we toured the *Arizona* a huge splendid ship. A sailor in an immaculate white uniform escorted us in groups over the ship, explaining the equipment and how it worked. After touring the upper deck we were directed to an opening in the deck with a ladder leading to the lower deck. The young sailor faced the opening and walked down the ladder quickly, but one at a time, the group of us went down the ladder backward the way we would at home.

The sailor smiled and waited patiently for us. On completing the tour we returned home with the knowledge of the supreme strength of our defense forces.

Then on December 7, 1941, the radio and newspapers gave us the news of the bombing of Pearl Harbor, and the *Arizona* was sunk. When we recall our tour, we wonder if our tour guide was one of the casualties.

Lucile Hebert
Yucaipa, California

Harbingers Of War

My vivid memories of 1941-1945 actually started a little before 1941. My mother and I visited her sister in El Dorado, Arkansas, in August 1940. One Sunday my uncle drove us to Shreveport, Louisiana. We saw a great building project going on — more buildings than we could count — at Barksdale Field.

That was the first that we could imagine the United States in another world war. My uncle had been a field orderly for a field Army hospital in France in World War I and was dumfounded that we were to get into another terrible war.

In August 1941 came another indication that our involvement was getting closer: the U.S./England Lend Lease Program. My hometown, Ponca City, Oklahoma, was selected as one of several training sites in the United States for a Darr School of Aeronautics.

We saw our first flight of British Empire pilot trainees. They arrived about every six weeks in groups of about 50. They came from all over the British Empire. On their first opportunity for weekend liberty, they all flocked to downtown Ponca in gray flannel double-breasted suits.

It didn't take long for townspeople to open their hearts and homes to all of them. I was 18 and in a business college as a student. We girls had great fun dating them. We danced, we picnicked and we went to the movies.

On December 7, 1941, I attended the Poncan Theatre with one of the cadets. As we walked the 15 blocks to my home for supper, we stopped at a cafe for hot chocolate.

That's when we learned Pearl Harbor had been bombed by Japan. My date was practically dancing on the table; as for me, I was like many in the room — stunned. But we all knew it meant the United States was in.

During that time, the Cuzalina's drugstore soda fountain was a popular place with cadets and dates. We Okies got a laugh when Mr. Cuzalina, who welcomed all who came, called to a group of cadets as they left the store, "Now you all come back." As a group, they turned and came back — right then!

Jane Curtis Waldroop
Norman, Oklahoma

Ensuring Fair Share

In the United States, rationing began a few days after the Japanese attack on Pearl Harbor on December 7, 1941, with a freeze on the sale of automobile tires. Before 1942 was over, other commodities followed, including automobiles, rubber footwear, coffee, sugar, gasoline, and fuel oil for heating.

After the defeat of Japan all rationing was lifted except sugar, which was controlled until June 1947. The decision to ration a commodity rested on the judgment of how scarce it was and how important. Rationing was begun to ensure that there would be a "fair share" for all consumers.

Ration coupons in books were issued for frequently purchased commodities such as gasoline, coffee and sugar. Local ration boards issued certificates for those commodities infrequently needed, such as tires.

Esther Carolus
Clarion, Iowa

Military Moves Quickly

The cultural aspects of the people of every part of the world were unalterably changed by the advent of hostilities in Europe. Especially after the Japanese attack on the United States Naval Station at Pearl Harbor and adjoining Army Air Corps bases near Honolulu. These specific events propelled the world's major nations into the greatest armed conflict in recorded history. I shall always remember the events immediately following that attack on December 7, 1941.

At the time, I was living in Seattle, an employee of the Boeing Airplane Company involved in the final assembly of the B-17 Flying Fortress.

All radio programs the day of December 7 were given to news that was related to what had taken place and directions that would be affecting us in the days to follow. A total blackout would be in effect from 10 p.m. until half an hour after sunrise. Also, all employees of the local defense industries were to report for work at their usual time.

These directives left an indelible impression upon me. One can hardly perceive how dark a big city can be or the difficulty in driving through the city in complete darkness. In the very early ghostly dawn, we could make out and were transfixed by the military encampment encompassing the plant.

Shortly before arrival at the factory, we were greeted by military personnel challenging us to produce proper identification. Approaching the factory entrance, we were challenged by machine-gun emplacements and instructed to come to authorized gates tomorrow or be subject to military action. After gaining access to the premises, we were kept out of the buildings until half an hour after sunrise to comply with blackout orders. This was the norm for several weeks.

From that time on, many major changes greeted us. The technological breakthroughs brought about during the War projected the world into civilization's most rapid advances ever experienced.

It is ironic that the world's greatest military struggle improved the overall welfare of the world's citizens.

Homer Nevermann
Seattle, Washington

History On The Radio

My World War II stories are not my parents, but my own. On May 2, 1941, my father was killed in a double traffic accident bringing me home from the Obert school where I taught. Late in the summer I got a call from Hubbell, Nebraska, asking me to come there to teach English and history. No teacher ever went back to Obert for a second year. I told the Hubbell superintendent I would come if they could find an apartment so my mother could live with me. We went. The apartment was created — in the home of nice people — from a large bedroom and oversized closet.

The last Christmas present from my father was a small radio with its own aerial. When we heard the news story of the bombing of Pearl Harbor, it was on that radio. When I went to school the next morning, I asked the superintendent to let me bring the radio to school so all of the pupils could hear President Franklin Delano Roosevelt's declaration of the United States' entry into World War II. The superintendent didn't believe I had a radio that I could carry to school and the whole school could hear. I did not have a car. It was the first time that the entire school had heard history being made by radio.

Guelda Shirley Jensen
Stanton, Nebraska

Never Too Late To Serve

My older brother and I were still attending school in the one-room schoolhouse where we earned our first eight years of education when Japan attacked Pearl Harbor on December 7, 1941. I can remember turning on the radio and hearing President Franklin D. Roosevelt saying that, "the only thing we have to fear is fear itself."

I can still see the sad face of our high school superintendent when his young son was killed in an air mission. The entire school was in mourning.

Before our high school years were finished the War ended, but our family knew the loneliness of having a loved family member missing when my brother was encouraged to join the Navy. At that time, a young man could complete the last semester of high school in the service. During those two years quite a few tears were shed by all of the family, including my brother, who was so homesick when he came home on leave he cried like a baby. He was so glad to be home.

When I was called to receive my diploma the night of graduation, the principal handed me my diploma and my brother's as I walked past. My brother was still in Key West, Florida, finishing up his training.

Rita Farnham
De Soto, Missouri

An Awful Surprise

I was sitting at the kitchen table on December 7, 1941, eating lunch with my 2- and 4-year-old sons when I learned what had happened. My brother-in-law brought home my 6-year-old daughter from the church Christmas program practice, and when he walked into the kitchen he exclaimed, "Do you know that the Japanese bombed Pearl Harbor?" I didn't have the radio on, so it was an awful surprise.

All my growing-up years, fear of the Japanese had been instilled in me. I don't recall why, but evidently they were a threat, making news in the daily paper that my parents often discussed.

Probably the most selfish thought that flashed through my mind was, "The money for buying Mother and Dad Boeckmann's farm won't be available now!" We were working with the government's Farm Home Administration to buy a farm from my husband's parents. But we were assured that the money was already allotted.

Over the next years, neighbors' sons were called into military service, and the boys in my high school class were also called to duty in both war theaters. I shed tears — and prayed.

Of course on the farm, food was plentiful, flour available. In the Midwest we were somewhat safe, and certainly blessed.

World War II ended on our 11th wedding anniversary, May 8, 1945.

Lucinda Boeckmann
Tripoli, Iowa

Pandemonium During Attack

I am a Pearl Harbor survivor who lived there at the time of the bombing. This is a short version of my experiences that day, December 7, 1941.

My husband was attached to a mine layer, the *USS Sicard* that laid mines in the waters around the islands. He was home two or three days a week.

Tensions had been growing with Japan, but no one suspected what was about to happen so soon. On Saturday, December 6, 1941, we went with our Portuguese neighbors, the Camaras, to spend the weekend in their beach home across Oahu and close to the Kaneoke Naval Air Station. That evening we were entertained by Hawaiian guitar players, who gave us beautiful Hawaiian music that lasted until 1 a.m.

Of course our 7-month-old baby did not sleep late the next morning. While I fed the baby, my husband and Bill Camara turned the radio on. It was so quiet there on that lovely beach. The radio suddenly interrupted the program with an urgent message for all civilian and military personnel to return to their stations immediately. "We are under a sporadic air attack," was being repeated and repeated, and they were saying, "Folks, this is not a joke, but the real thing." The fellows thought it was no doubt a drill and turned the radio off. Just then a Japanese plane, with the rising sun under its wing, flew over us towards the Kaneoke Air Station.

That convinced us it was no joke, so we hurriedly loaded up and headed back to Honolulu. Because the men were not in uniform, we were detained for identification as we crossed the Pali. From there we could see the whole of Pearl Harbor, and our hearts sank! As we drove on, we saw a body being carried from a house that had been strafed, as well as a car that had been hit with the bodies still in it.

It was pandemonium on Dillingham Boulevard, the main street that we lived off of, and we had to run the last two blocks to get to our house. Neither I or my husband could ever remember who carried the suitcase and who carried the baby. Neighbors yelled at us as we ran, with mostly true reports of ships sunk, etc.

No one knew for a while about the terrible devastation and the loss of over 2,000 men. The Japanese did not know how badly they had crippled us. They could have taken the island.

My husband, Iden, quickly got into uniform and went down the street. He was picked up by a policeman and taken to his ship, which was in overhaul, but not hit. I did not see him until Thursday; a detachment from the ship had located all the families on Tuesday.

Martial law was declared immediately, with complete blackout. Not even a pinpoint of light could show. Soon we could get heavy black paper to blacken out at least one room. No unauthorized person was allowed out on the street after dark. It was scary to hear footsteps outside a window in your yard — and even hear rifle fire, which we hoped was practice.

It was over a week before we could get any messages to families on the mainland. My folks read in the newspaper that the baby and I were missing. I got word to them that we were alive! Rumors ran wild. Our water had been poisoned! It was only a rumor.

Schools were closed and became Red Cross Centers to make bandages and provide emergency help. Blood was badly needed. All we heard on the radio were instructions for the people and any war news they could tell us .

Anytime unidentified aircraft approached the island an air-raid siren went off. The shelters in our area were huge cement tubes behind our building. We had to carry gas masks at all times and had an emergency kit ready in case of another attack.

I received orders to be evacuated by December 31. That was canceled, and one evening in mid-March 1942, sheets of paper were handed out at every door for 2,000 military dependents to be at Honolulu Harbor by 8 the next morning. My baby and I were put on the *Aquatania*, a British first-class liner that had been converted to a troop ship to carry troops between San Francisco and Australia. We were in a convoy with U.S. destroyers as escorts until we reached safe waters. We had one submarine scare and many lifeboat drills. The Church of England held services on Sunday and we had tea on deck every day at 4 p.m.

Everyone was on deck as we sailed into San Francisco Bay. With heavy hearts, we were happy to be back in the United States. We were also sad to have left loved ones, not knowing if we would ever see them again.

Pearle M. Nash
Wichita, Kansas

No Sleepy Sunday

Printed in *Grit*, December 7, 1992.

Our furnished one-room apartment was unfamiliar to me.

I slowly turned over and my back touched the warm body next to me. I reached out and switched on the radio to some sleepy Sunday morning music. It was December 7, 1941.

Without warning, a crackling of static interrupted, and "Japan has attacked United States," blared out.

I sat right up in bed. How could a tiny island such as Japan attack a country of such enormity as the United States? It must be a joke like the "War of the Worlds," a program by Orson Welles.

Bill awakened and drowsily said, "What's going on?"

"Pearl Harbor is being bombed by Japan," I said.

"I don't believe it," said Bill.

I turned to Bill and said, "I'm not even used to being married yet. The world can't do this to us." Stunned disbelief, anger, frustration and anxiety took over our thoughts.

"It can't be true," I remarked. But it was!

Ruth Carroll Foster
East Hartford, Connecticut

No More Routines

"It's time to get up, Shirley!" How I hated to throw back the covers and run through the cold room and downstairs to the living room. I wanted Mother to braid my hair before she left for work because it had to be just right — I was an extremely tidy child.

Mother and Dad worked in Chestertown at the newly opened defense plant. Before they left for work, Sallie, our sitter, would come. "Call your sisters," she would say, "or you all will miss the bus." We had to be at the end of the short driveway, or the driver would go right by without stopping. He was elderly, and had very thick glasses; nowadays he wouldn't be permitted to drive. We had to cross a railroad track, and all the children knew they had better help him look for the train.

We arrived home one afternoon to find Mother and Dad both home early. They told us a storage shed had exploded, killing several people at the plant. They and quite a few others had quit that day. Mother did assembly line work that involved capping explosive devices. Dad probably had a similar job. Soon after that Dad went to work at a shipyard in Cambridge, and Mother stayed home and became a housewife again.

School was no longer routine. Any hour of the day the air-raid siren would sound and the teacher would say, "Line up children, and be quick." We would be herded across the street to a garage and squeezed in with mechanics, tools and several cars to wait for the "all clear."

We could purchase savings stamps, and when our books were filled they were exchanged for a U.S. Savings Bond.

Once a week we rode our bicycles five miles to a farm near Queenstown where Mother was a volunteer plane spotter. She had to call in and identify every plane that flew over her territory.

The day Pearl Harbor was attacked I remember vividly. I walked home across a field between my house and my grandparents' farmhouse all alone. I wanted to listen to my favorite radio program. It was interrupted by a speech by President Roosevelt telling about the attack by the Japanese. At the age of 9 I knew exactly what the president meant when he said, "This day will go down in infamy."

Shirley Daffin
Easton, Maryland

Isolated No More

Once again, the sound of marching feet could be heard throughout the world.

In 1939 the United States was still trying to free itself from the effects of the Great Depression. Although things were better, close to 10 million people remained unemployed. The country had for a decade turned inward as government and private citizens alike struggled with economic problems. The trend was isolationistic.

By this time radio commentators, such as H.V. Kaltenborn, were reporting such things as Japan was on the march, and Hitler would never be satisfied until he controlled all of Europe. Ordinary Americans reacted to Hitler's conquest of Europe with apprehension that at times approached panic. The feeling was that if Great Britain fell, Germans might invade America.

It was the Japanese, however, who plunged the country into war. On that Sunday, December 7, 1941, as people were eating dinner and the radio was playing "Swing and Sway" with Sammy Kaye, the announcer broke in with the news report. "Today, Japanese have attacked Pearl Harbor, Hawaii, from the air — a second attack has been reported on Army and Navy bases in Manila." The attack on Pearl Harbor, in which more than 2,400 Americans died and half the Pacific Fleet was wiped out, canceled all isolationistic feelings and unified the United States more than any war it ever fought.

The War solved most Depression-related problems, giving employment to seven million people who were out of work. Nearly eight million more women, teenagers and older people found work, many for the first time in their lives. Women took on tough, dirty, boring jobs: riveting airplanes, tanks and ships; shoveling coal; making bullets and war-time products. Automobile makers turned out planes and tanks. For three years no new cars came out.

Farmers, the group hardest hit through the Depression, saw their incomes triple. People spent more money in nightclubs and restaurants. Trains were jammed with soldiers and people rushing to meet servicemen on leave. Businessmen hurried to Washington and Chicago to help the nation gear up for war.

Troop trains went through our small Midwest Iowa town. It was sad but exciting to see all those uniformed men leaning out of the windows and waving as they passed by. I always shed a few tears afterward, and I felt such pride for all those young men, who were all about my age.

Esther Carolus
Clarion, Iowa

"I'll Be Back"

I was a senior student nurse on duty, December 7, 1941, at St. Joseph's Hospital, in Keokuk, Iowa. We were serving trays for the Sunday evening meal. I was dashing in and out of rooms when I heard on the radio that the Japanese had bombed Pearl Harbor. The announcer sounded very excited and confident that war would be imminent. Chills ran up my spine as I thought of my two oldest brothers — plus cousins and friends — being of draft age. I wondered about the boys who had enlisted for a year and had expected to be home soon. Their enlistment would probably be extended. I thought of the song, "I'll Be Back in a Year, Little Darling."

The next morning we heard the news, "F.D.R. declares War!" It was official. We were at war!

Soon we were issued war ration books. Sacrifices must be made at home to take care of the military. Gasoline, tires, shoes, sugar, coffee, cigarettes and butter were rationed. We could not buy nylon hose. Ladies wore "painted" hose or cotton "service weight" stockings. Nearly everyone had a victory garden planted in every small area available. We were urged to buy War Bonds. My oldest brother was inducted in February 1942.

After my graduation, I was on special duty with a young Coast Guard serviceman who had become very ill while stationed at the Keokuk Dam. I earned $10 a day for 20-hour duty. This was a lot of money at that time. The servicemen were paid only $25 a month. My dad worked for $3 a day. When my patient was transferred to the U.S. Marine Hospital in St. Louis, I was asked to go as a nurse escort on the train. I was given a tour of the hospital and a job offer. I loved it! We had nice accommodations with a good salary. The patients were servicemen in the Coast Guard, Navy and Merchant Marines.

However, in less than a year, I was transferred from the U.S. Public Health Service to Immigration and Naturalization Service and was sent to an Alien Internment Camp in Crystal City, Texas. I had no choice. Uncle Sam gave the orders. The camp was for families living in the United States without citizenship, whose country we were at war with. Japanese families lived on one side of the camp. German families on the other. They each had their own little house. Many planted small gardens and flower beds. They were given work inside the camp. Many worked in the hospital. The camp was surrounded by a high fence with guard stations at each corner. Mounted patrol guards rode horseback around the fence. The nurse quarters was a barracks outside the big gate. We carried an ID card to show each time we went in or out of the camp.

In the meantime, I had a brother in New Guinea and another in

North Africa. I became dissatisfied, but did tough it out several months before I joined the Army. My parents were under so much stress and concern for my brothers, and they didn't want me to join.

I took my basic training at Camp Carson, Colorado. We had a tough drill sergeant with many hash marks on his sleeve. We were on the drill field at sunup, dressed in fatigues, ready to do push ups, march right, left, about face, etc. His delight was telling us how sloppy we were! Then it was "double time" to the mess hall and classroom. Our new shoes killed our feet! We learned how to wear a gas mask and then were tested in a gas chamber. We took a 10-mile hike up the mountain with an ambulance following. Flag etiquette and other military regulations were taught in the classroom. After basic I was sent to the hospital in Fort Riley, Kansas.

On V. J. Day, August 14, 1945, when the Japanese surrendered, I had four brothers, a brother-in-law, my husband-to-be and myself in service. The good news was everyone would soon be coming home! I was married while still in the service.

Rovilla Landry
Kerrville, Texas

"Goodbye Dear"

Conscription had been discontinued after the Armistice in 1918 and reinstituted in the Selective Training and Service Act of 1940, the first United States peacetime draft. All males 21-35 were required to register with their local draft boards. A lottery by drawing in Washington, D.C., selected those for training and service. They were to serve for one year, but in August of 1941, it was extended to 18 months.

October 29, 1940, as a band played and planes flew overhead, the first draft numbers in America's first peacetime military draft were drawn by Secretary of War Henry L. Stimson. They were drawn from a bowl.

Men in each Selective Service area in the nation whose numbers corresponded to those drawn from the bowl were called up for a year of service in the Army. When the United States entered the War, the age limits were expanded from 18 to 65, though only 20 to 45 year olds were eligible for the service. The period was then extended to the duration of the War plus six months.

On December 7, 1941, Japanese planes attacked Pearl Harbor. On December 8, President Roosevelt declared war against Japan and Germany, and December 11, against Italy. So now it was a global conflict between the Axis Powers — Germany, Italy, Japan and satellites — and the Allies — the United States, Great Britain France, Russia and China. It lasted from 1939 to 1945.

There was a popular song written that year about men being drafted for just one year of training:

Goodbye dear,
I'll be back in a year
Don't forget
That I love you.

Before that year was up we were at war, so some of these boys didn't get home until the end of it.

During the war, as small as our little town was, we lost four of our young men. Our town's population was about 90 at that time.

Esther Carolus
Clarion, Iowa

———■———

50

Chapter 3: The Perils Of War

Two Generations Of Sacrifice

Shortly before his 19th birthday, my brother was killed in Guadalcanal by a sniper.

I remember the day my parents received the telegram informing them of Jim's death. My mother looked at the back of the envelope and there was the dreaded gold star. More than 50 years have passed, but I can still close my eyes and hear my mother's cries.

My father was 45 at the time and vowed to avenge the death of his eldest son. Because of his age he was turned down by every branch of the service. He managed to enlist in the Seabees just before enlistments were closed, and was sent to the South Pacific. There he helped to pave the road back to the Philippines for Gen. MacArthur.

He was wounded atop a bulldozer and sent to a base hospital. While recuperating he had the privilege of visiting Jim's grave at Henderson Field in Guadalcanal.

Alice Williams

Humphreys, Missouri

Joyous Reunion On Battlefield

While my husband was in Germany with the 908th Field Artillery, he saw this happen.

There were two brothers who met. Each was in a separate unit. One of the brothers noticed the identification of the other unit and knew it was one his brother was with. He went to them and asked for his brother, not knowing if he was still alive or not.

They went and got him, and when they saw each other, they put their arms around each other and wept with joy that each was still alive.

Zelma Scott
Roach, Missouri

Tree Testimonial

East of St. Lo, France, we got started. There was a colonel at the fortress of St. Malo called the "mad colonel" who didn't want to surrender, and to the east were 20,000 armed German soldiers who didn't want to surrender either. That is, they didn't want to until the 83rd Division, my division, came along.

Col. Von Aubock was the defiant commander who decided to hold out. For a while it looked as if he would, but the "Thunderbolt" Division laid siege to his stronghold and changed his mind for him. In that battle I caught a lump of exploded shell in the right knee. It was buried in the bone — more than a flesh wound — so I had to go over to England for proper treatment.

In England I was located at a place named Ragley Hall in Warwickshire. During my recuperation period I walked about the grounds at Ragley. One day I used my Scout knife to carve "U.S.A., R.A.J., 1944" in a tree some distance from the main building used as a hospital by U.S. medics.

I must have done a good job of carving, because on June 15, 1987, I was invited by the Marquess of Hertford, the Lord of Ragley Hall, to come to Warwickshire for a ceremonial removal of that tree because it had become diseased. Forty- three years after I had recuperated in the medical center of Ragley Hall, I was invited by the owner, Lord Hugh Edward Seymour, Marquess of Hertford, to come spend a day with him.

Robert A. Johnson
McCain, North Carolina

"Hang On"

83rd Spearhead
Somewhere in Germany
March 24, 1945

"Remember to hang on. Whatever you do, hang on while riding the tanks," cautioned the sergeant from Company L, 331st Infantry. "That's the only way I can be sure of having you all when the fireworks start."

The attack opened, and the doughs held on. But when they looked around for their sergeant, he was gone. He had fallen off.

Zelma Scott
Roach, Missouri

Kokomo Veteran Bags 10 Enemy Planes

This is an excerpt from a newspaper interview with Staff Sgt. James W. Wisler.

"Staff Sgt. James W. Wisler, who has bagged 10 enemy planes and several more 'possibles,' thinks the answer to the comparatively light German aerial resistance in France may be that the Nazis are conserving what air power they have left to make a last-ditch defense of the Fatherland.

"Sgt. Wisler, home in Kokomo (Indiana) on furlough after his outstanding record as a tail gunner on a B-24 Liberator bomber based in Italy, said Saturday that the command to which he was attached always ran into more Nazi fighter planes near the German border than over Italy, Rumania, France or other countries, indicating that the dwindling Luftwaffe was saving its strength for a final stand over its own soil.

"The boyish sergeant, who is 23 years old and modest about his experiences, flew on 50 missions before he was sent home on furlough. His crew shot down 14 German planes, and he received credit for 10 of them.

"The missions Sgt. Wisler's plane took part in were over the

Ploesti oil fields in Munich, Germany — which he helped bomb twice — Vienna, Toulon and Lyon in France, Bucharest, Budapest, Campini in Rumania, and other places. None of the members of his crew was wounded on any of the 50 missions. The plane caught plenty of flak, too — one day it came home with 218 bullet and cannon holes, and on five successive trips, one of its motors was shot out.

"Sgt. Wisler counts the raids over the Ploesti oil reserve as the most dangerous he made. On one of these attacks, his plane caught fire and dropped out of formation, and the bomber behind them also dropped out. Nazi fighters swarmed in and got the bomber trailing Wisler's ship.

"'Then they made one pass at us, and flew away,' Wisler said. 'We were lucky. If they had come in again, they probably would have got us, for all of us were about out of ammunition. I had seven or eight rounds left for my two .50 calibre machine-guns.'

"In one air battle, he said, his two guns became overheated and both cut out. He saw two German fighters coming in at his position and was helpless to strike back at them. But he told his pilot, and the latter swung the Liberator about so that the waist gunner could get the Germans in his sights. This gunner knocked down one of the Nazis and the other fled."

Pauline Wisler
Niceville, Florida

Preparation For D-Day

My dad told me about his war stories when I was younger. He was in the U.S. Army, and after basic training, he went to school for motorcycle mechanics and clerk typing school. He was in the 293rd MM Company, which is a medium maintenance ordnance company. My dad, George Smith, went overseas in March 1943 to Europe.

He tells me they landed in Glasgow, Scotland, then went south in England to a little town named Cutting Corners. Then his company moved south to Dorchester, England, where his company was feeding and billeting the infantry land tanks waiting before the D-Day invasion.

Day after day, airplanes would fly over the English Channel to France, bombing the German positions. There were a lot of balloons in the harbor to keep airplanes from France and Germany from strafing the harbor. One night when the bombers were returning, some German planes followed them back. The searchlights went on, and anti-aircraft guns shot them down.

He said one day after a heavy two- or three-day rainstorm, there was a lot of activity in the harbor. A lot of soldiers and equipment were loaded on large barge-like LSTs. For the next few weeks, ships were leaving the harbor. He didn't know it at the time, but it was D-Day, when Eisenhower made the big push into France.

John E. Smith
League City, Texas

"This One Shot My Buddy"

I want to tell you something a soldier told me.

"I never thought I could deliberately kill a defenseless human being," he said, "but that was before a sniper got my buddy in Normandy.

"My buddy was just a young kid. He had gotten off on the wrong foot when he first came to the Army and had been court-martialed several times back in the States. One day I went to the C.O. and told him that everyone was down on the kid and just watching for him to do something else wrong. That was why he was still in trouble all the time.

"If you'll just see that he is given a chance," he said, "I think he'll make a good soldier yet!"

"All right," said the C.O. "He is probationed to your care. See what you can do with him."

"Sure enough, the kid straightened out and finally became one of the most respected men in the company. Realizing that I had helped him to get a break, he couldn't do enough for me. We became as brothers.

"Then one day in Normandy, it happened. We were advancing across a supposedly cleared area when a hidden sniper shot my buddy through the spine. He died in about 15 minutes. Then I was determined to get that sniper.

"I started crawling across the ground in the direction from which the shot had come. Soon I had the sniper's position located. Inch-by-inch I crept nearer.

"Then suddenly, the spy stood up, hands in the air, holding a white cloth of surrender. He was not more than 20 feet away. I shot him right between the eyes.

"I had thought that I could never kill a defenseless human being, but this one had shot my buddy and tried to save himself by surrender."

Beatrice E. Tucker
Oklahoma City, Oklahoma

"We Felt Like Sitting Ducks"

Let me take you for a ride on the Red Ball Highway in 1944.

"Meyer, where the heck are you?" my first sergeant called.

He probably could have been heard in two countries. He was a large man with a mighty voice that carried lots of weight when we were in combat. In civilian life, he had been an auctioneer.

We were nearly through Belgium, low on ammunition and fuel. Gen. Patton was calling for more. We'd been told we probably wouldn't advance much farther for another two weeks. Everything was real quiet.

We were told to stay armed, but we were allowed to wander a reasonable distance from our command post. My best friend was from upstate New York and he spoke French as well as the natives. We were a couple of miles into the countryside and met a young couple who invited us to a steak supper at their home. It was hard

five apartments. The owner stored all his furniture on the third floor. I loved the big maples in the yard and the bay windows in the house. I asked the woman in charge if I might put my name on the waiting list. She said I'd be about number 20.

Seeing my friend's dog the woman exclaimed, "You didn't tell me you had a dog. I can't have a dog in here." Turning to me, she asked if we had a dog. I assured her we didn't. "Then you can have the apartment," she said.

Although we didn't have any furniture, I paid the rent right then. We moved in a day or two later. It was here that we had our first victory garden. Each tenant was given several rows in the garden to plant and work vegetables of his choice. I grew up in the country, and the gardening was fun for me. The couple next to us was from New York City, and they had a lot to learn.

About the time the snap beans were ready to pick, Japanese beetles moved into the garden. Overnight they ate all the leaves off the okra stalks. Bare stems were thick with beetles the next day. My husband got orders to be transferred immediately to another camp and our garden was forgotten.

Gypsy Damaris Boston
Shreveport, Louisiana

Precious Memories

In 1944, I traveled from my hometown of Elmer, New Jersey, to Cameron Valley, Virginia, with our blond, blue-eyed, 2-year-old Ernie, to be with my husband, Aaron. A technical sergeant with the Quartermaster Corps of Fort Belvior, he left for the European theater four months later.

Our government offered a six-month training course for nursery school teachers, and I enrolled in Alexandria, where I had rented an apartment. Six months of a grueling schedule in a city filled with soot and grime, plus contagious childhood diseases rampant in the academy Ernie attended, played havoc on Ernie's health. Concerned friends invited us to sample life in Santa Fe, New Mexico. Our friends

June and Bernie Fry met our yellow school bus at the end of The Old Santa Fe Trail. During our three-week visit, I inquired about employment at local nursery schools. No one was hiring. Then Lady Luck smiled upon us. A wealthy family needed a substitute for their vacationing governess. I qualified, and agreed to the live-in arrangement, which included Ernie, for one month. We got along famously with 4-year-old Alex Bonnyman, a charmer.

Soon it would be time to move on. Where?

Not unlike my beloved Granddad Flitcraft, my destination would be California. Amid tears, we bid all friends goodbye and took a taxi to the Greyhound bus terminal. Three days and three nights later, I watched bleary-eyed as the bus pulled into the Los Angeles depot at 4 a.m.

I limped toward an agent's window to inquire about a hotel in the City of Angels and accepted the only reservation available. The hotel, a seedy affair, stood in a questionable section of the city. War regulations stated we must be out by 9 a.m. (with less than three hours sleep). We found ourselves gaping at palms and smelling flowers in the early morning sunshine.

Finally, we settled with a North Hollywood family, Russell Horton, wife Gladys, Russ Jr., four, and Madalyn, two.

Several months passed before I became uneasy and decided it was time to move on. We moved to Beverly Hills, to a cottage on the grounds of a private school in need of a kindergarten teacher. Ernie would attend the nursery school.

Our neighbor, Mr. Willet, frequently visited the school with his collie, Pal, in tow. The three homes now housing the Eunice Knight Saunders School had been previously owned by him. They had been gifts to his bride, Miss Billie Dove, the beautiful blonde actress of silent films.

One morning as he walked about with his Brownie camera, Mr. Willet met us on our way to the schoolyard. He invited us into his yard, where he took snapshots of Ernie with Pal, who was Lassie, of *Lassie Come Home* and other films.

A whirlwind of activities took place during the two weeks spent in Beverly Hills. The War ended. Aaron, via V-Mail, said he'd come home and to wait for him in New Jersey. I joined others in a parade in Hollywood. Homeward bound, we said goodbye to what might have been. With precious snapshots, happy memories never wear out.

Evelyn L. Botbyl
Wilmington, Delaware

A Wartime Christmas Memory

The United States was at war. Nobody felt much like celebrating, but when we were together at Thanksgiving in the home of Aunt Gladys and Uncle John, Uncle John brought out the Sears Roebuck Catalog and a pen. He said, "I'm going to pass this around. I want everyone to find something you want for Christmas and write your name beside it in this catalog."

"What in the world?" I thought. "Uncle John must have a hidden gold mine. How else could he think of giving every one of us what we want?"

In spite of the puzzlement, we took up the challenge and had a great time deciding just where to write our names.

When Christmas finally came, we were together again. Uncle John, Aunt Gladys and their family were the last to arrive. They were loaded down with carefully wrapped packages.

As always there was the traditional meal, cleanup, and singing of carols. Then it was gift passing time. There were some real gift exchanges that year because we drew names to see for whom we should buy a gift. After those gifts were passed out, Uncle John started to distribute the gifts he had brought. What excitement!

Each elaborately wrapped package held the catalog picture with a name written on or beside it. Whatever you wrote your name on you got, along with a piece of candy, a stick of gum or some other small token of love.

Lois Denham
Sioux City, Iowa

Going Where The Work Is

In 1941 we lived on a farm in Elbert County, Colorado, and that year our crops got hailed out. I had two brothers in California, and they suggested we come out there and get a job. We had a public sale, packed our personal possessions in a two-wheel trailer, and left on December 9, two days after Pearl Harbor.

Since war had been declared, my husband had no trouble getting a job at Douglas Aircraft in Long Beach, where my brothers also worked.

Sometimes, when we were coming home from visiting my brothers in Los Angeles, there would be servicemen hitching rides back to the bases in Long Beach. Often we would pick them up. We met many nice boys and enjoyed talking to them very much — we could never do that nowadays, which is very sad.

At one of the schools, they would have the registration for the ration books. They needed help, so I volunteered once. It was interesting. One day, I was registering an epileptic man, and he had a seizure. It caused some excitement, but he came out of it OK.

When the War was over, we promptly packed up and went back to Colorado to start farming again. That lasted until 1954. When our crops got wiped out again, we moved to Englewood, and then finally to Commerce City where we have lived ever since.

Esther Tweden
Commerce City, Colorado

Doing One's Part

"You had it so easy — you didn't have to go to war." How many times did we hear this from returning servicemen? You can bet we were working as hard as they, although we weren't on the front lines. As teenagers, my husband and I helped on the farm, putting up hay, helping to harvest the grain. We also picked up scrap metal, walked to school, carpooled and bought bonds with any loose money we had. We were doing our part too.

The Plummers
Osawatomie, Kansas

A True Soldier On The Home Front

How does one put into words the cataclysmic event that burst upon our lives as unsuspecting young parents?

Ed Baker, my dear husband of many years, and I lived in Cincinnati. Our first baby, a son named Michael, was only a few weeks old when Pearl Harbor was attacked on the "Day of Infamy," December 7, 1941. When the news came, Ed and I were on our first outing since the birth, while my mother cared for our infant son.

We had been to a movie — the title long since forgotten — and were in the car on our way home. We were listening to lively, cheerful music on the car radio. Suddenly there was an interruption. The United States had declared war and entered the conflagration that came to be known as World War II!

We hardly knew what that meant at the time and carried on our lives as usual. Of course, my husband was registered with the draft board, but he had not been called. Ed was a newspaper circulation manager and had been offered a new job as circulation representative for Marshall Field's new paper, *The Chicago Sun*. He traveled throughout Ohio and surrounding states, including West Virginia. It was lonely at home without Ed, but it was a lucrative job. We were able to save $1,100, which served as the down payment when we bought our first home.

At Christmastime in 1942, while I was dressed in my new blue velvet dress and eating a piece of expensive fruit cake, I got a phone call from Ed. He told me that his newspaper job had folded, a victim of war-related cutbacks. Somehow that fruit cake lost its luscious taste, and my blue velvet dress lost its luster!

Ed decided to look for "War work." He had no experience except in the newspaper business. He answered a classified ad for a factory job that stated, "Will train green labor." Ed applied, and came home jubilant from the interview. "I got a job on the night shift, and they'll pay me 55 cents an hour!"

Thus Ed entered the blue-collar world. He outfitted himself with work clothes and boots. We acquired a tin lunch box with a

Thermos bottle, and I learned to pack a working man's lunch. All during the war years, Ed worked 12 hours a night, six nights a week, at 55 cents an hour.

Now for a smile. When Ed reported for work the first time, he learned that his employer was not the company that had advertised, but the factory next door. He had been so excited at getting a job that he signed up without paying attention to the employer's name. The company that hired Ed manufactured valves, many of which were huge ones used in ships. Ed was given a treasured memento, a red-and-blue lapel pin with a silver star, issued by the Wartime Commission of the United States. It was engraved "Award of Merit," and "Ships for Victory," on a silver eagle, wings outspread.

During the war years, I gained a new, and deeper respect for my husband. He, who was used to setting his own hours and had never so much as driven a nail or done manual labor, exhibited qualities I never dreamed he had. His loyalty, humility and stick-to-it-ness were above reproach. I'm proud of his contribution to the war effort. He did not serve overseas, but he certainly helped win the war.

Marcia Baker Pogue
Cincinnati, Ohio

Dear Soldier

After school was out for the summer of 1942, several teenage girls discovered that every evening at 9 p.m., a troop train stopped for water at our railroad station. The servicemen couldn't leave the train, but they had their windows open. We would gather up old magazines around the town, write our names and addresses in them, then hand the magazines through the windows. Soon we all began to get letters from everywhere there was a military post.

Several of us were getting letters from the same tank outfit stationed in Louisiana. We fantasized that at the end of the War, we would see a row of tanks coming down the road toward our little village in the Oklahoma Panhandle, bringing the fellows we had been corresponding with. Of course this didn't happen, and soon we didn't hear from any of them.

After the war one soldier returned and married the girl who had been writing to him. None of the rest of us received serious letters. They usually ended with, "Your Pen Pal."

During the same time we began to hear a radio program called "Dear Soldier." Girls were encouraged to write a letter, and send it to the radio station, where it would be passed on to a soldier who wanted to correspond. I received a letter from a private first class, and we corresponded throughout the War. I could tell by his letters that he was educated and more mature than the others I wrote to. He was stationed in the Aleutian Islands and wrote such interesting letters that I have kept them.

One day after the War ended and we had moved to central Oklahoma, where I was attending college, Jim came to visit for the weekend. He took me out to eat and to a movie. The next day Mom invited him to dinner. We continued to correspond occasionally.

I did my part for the war by writing to other soldiers and sailors who were cousins or brothers of mine and my friends.

Betty J. French
Mercedes, Texas

Livestock Provided Well

During World War II, gasoline was rationed, as was coffee, sugar and several other things. We lived on a farm and had eggs to sell, but they were only 11 cents a dozen and at times hard to sell.

My husband worked at the Marathon filling station, and they had to have ration stamps to get gasoline. My daughters worked in town and rented an apartment there because of gasoline rationing. We had a garden, milk cows, and hogs and chickens, so we didn't go hungry.

Lillian Stewart
Marshall, Illinois

Stamping Out The Enemy

After 40 years I still have some vivid memories of World War II. My Dad was fighting in the War I was living with my grandma in rural Ontario, Canada.

We all wanted to do our part to help win the War. I used to daydream about flying a plane over Hitler's house and dropping a bomb on him. I was sure that would put an end to the War, and I would be a hero.

We all wished we could wipe out the enemy. Our teacher gave us coupon books with pictures of Hitler and Mussolini drawn on the pages. We would bring in a certain amount of change and were given a stamp to cover a portion of their faces. The object was to stamp out (cover up) the entire face of the enemy. The money collected was sent to the war effort.

Every evening, chores done, Grandma and I would listen to all the war news on the radio. We tried to figure out if my father was in the area of all the casualties. It was hard to grasp the enormity of it. There were no vivid TV pictures showing the human suffering.

One day I was at a friend of my grandma's, rewaxing her hardwood floors. There was a commotion at her back door, and when I looked up, there stood my dad. He was safe; he was home. I nearly knocked him over when I ran into his arms. I learned much later that Dad was home before the end of the war because like so many men, he had contracted malaria overseas. He had brought me a wonderful gift, a bicycle. I learned to ride it by getting on a knoll and pushing off. Because rubber was needed for the war effort, the bike had wooden wheels. That did not matter to me. What mattered was my dad was home from the war, he was safe.

Noma J. Boyle
Pine Mountain Club, California

No Parts Available

On the home front our lives went on much as usual. My husband farmed, and we had two small babies, so he was not drafted. I can't remember the rationing being too much of a hardship. We had always canned a lot of fruit, and we were short of sugar for that. Some people used saccharin — a diabetic sweetener — but we thought it gave the fruit a bitter taste, and I just made a lighter syrup on ours.

We did have one problem with shortages. We were not able to get repair parts. We had a new gas washing machine that we had gotten in 1938 when we were married, our one luxury in those Depression days. Something went wrong with it, and no one had the part on hand, so we couldn't get it fixed for the duration of the War. I washed by hand on the scrub board, and about every two weeks took my wash to my mother's, a 30-mile round trip away.

The better prices and demand for food following the Depression due to World War II made life so much easier. It was with a feeling of guilt that we realized our scale of living was so much better at the cost of the suffering and dying of our servicemen overseas.

My brother in Italy was in my thoughts and prayers constantly. One night I had a dream. I saw a troop of men with heavy packs on their backs climbing up a hill in mud. I was standing there watching them and crying. Suddenly, one of the men turned and looked at me. I saw it was my brother, and he was smiling. I had never put much faith in dreams, but for some reason that dream gave me a feeling of peace. From then on I had faith that my brother would be home safely. I felt that God had touched me and answered my constant prayers.

Our family was of German descent. People were so angry at anything German that I would not have mentioned that we were German for anything. I was new in the community so did not know anyone's background, but they were always talking about people who they thought were German sympathizers. My parents had both been American-born, but feelings really ran high through these years.

Esther Carolus
Clarion, Iowa

Christmas Memories

I wasn't quite 3 years old when World War II began, so my wartime memories are those of a child. What I remember most about those years is Christmas. Trying to make a celebration must have been hard for our parents, but I don't recall the hardships, only the warmth and fun of family and community gatherings and celebrations.

I do remember my mother wishing for simple things, such as tree decorations in the stores, wrapping paper and ribbon, tinsel, even tape, but since I couldn't remember or imagine such items, I didn't feel deprived in the least. Our tree was decorated with pop-corn and cranberry strings and colorful paper chains. The metal strips from coffee cans were pulled out into a shiny spiral and hung by the key. One year, even construction paper for chains couldn't be found, so my sister and I colored and cut strips of toilet paper.

The high point of the day was the family Christmas dinner, held each year at the home of one relative or another. My mother would be cooking early Christmas morning, because dinner, of course, was pot-luck. It was pot-luck that involved a whole lot of planning and many telephone calls because of shortages and food rationing. Meat was no problem, as lots of the families were farm-ing. Everyone raised big gardens then, so home-canned vegetables were plentiful and delicious, and every family dinner featured at least a half-dozen varieties of pickles.

I wish I could remember how on earth those women contrived to make cakes and pies; somehow they did, and I think a lot of the telephone calls I remember dealt with who had enough of which scarce ingredient to provide a special treat.

The last event of the day and of the season was the gift exchange, held in time for the farmers to get home and complete farm chores at least partly in the daylight. Everyone attending had a gift from the person who had drawn his or her name. A quart jar of home-canned fruit with real sugar or some homemade jelly were welcome gifts. A carton of cigarettes for a smoker, obtained with a non-smoker's ration points, was one present sometimes given, as was a pound of coffee.

I wouldn't willingly return to those years, which were so difficult and fearful for the adults who lived through them, but I will always marvel at the hard work, resourcefulness and sacrifice of those who made my childhood a smiling, sunlit time.

Carol Wells
Havensville, Kansas

Creativity In The Kitchen

My first memory of World War II was when a friend's daughter, her husband and little daughter visited in Minnesota. The young husband was a Naval member. He returned to duty on the West Coast, leaving his family in Minnesota. Soon the wife received a telegram: "For heaven's sake stay where you are." The Japanese had bombed Pearl Harbor.

Then followed rationing. We were farmers, and had our own dairy products as well as garden produce. We did not need coupons for food, except sugar. For farmers 10 pounds was insufficient, for farmers often had extra men to feed.

Long before mixes came on the market, I developed my own. I had cake mixes, canned syrup for fruit canning — we were limited to only 40 cans of fruit. I decided to can in water-pack and discovered a little salt cut the tartness of applesauce and some other fruits. I made ice cream with saccharin. Corn syrup was available, and we learned to use it in baking especially. Molasses and honey were easy to find and substitute for sugar.

Our most difficult problem was gas and fuel oil shortages. Our furnace burned diesel fuel and we could not get enough to warm that uninsulated Minnesota house. Our son was a tiny baby, so we bought a coal-burning heater and installed it in the living room.

Hazel Wilson
Mountain View, California

Better Use For Hemp

We were just coming out of a Depression when the War started, so people weren't wealthy, but our 10-cent corn soon soared to $2. Farmers and businessmen alike prospered. One day farmers received a penny postcard in the mail stating "Rope is scarce. The farmers need it, and our boys in the service need it. It is your patriotic duty to grow hemp." Many farmers signed contracts to grow hemp to make twine and rope. Years later, when we found hemp growing wild in the ditches, people learned it could be harvested as marijuana.

Our local hatchery hired Japanese men to sex the baby chicks, because they were faster and better at it. When the War broke out, all Japanese suddenly became our enemies and the men in town kept a 24-hour surveillance on them until they finished their work and left town.

The newspaper office sent copies of the local newspaper to subscribers in Norway. They had always gone through, but when the War started, the papers were returned with a notation on the wrapper "Not Passed By Censor." Inside was this message: "This communication returned to sender because it is addressed to an enemy or enemy-occupied country. Personal messages may be sent through the Red Cross."

Jeanette Larson
Story City, Iowa

On The Road For The War Effort

My mom, Lona Curtis, has told me some things about the way they lived during the World War II era. My mom and dad had just lived through the Depression years when many people were unemployed. My dad had built a nice house trailer to live in so they could go from job to job. When he heard of a powder plant to be built in Millington, Tennessee, near Memphis, that's where they went. Daddy was a steam fitter.

There was no trailer park there, so the trailer was parked near a farmer's home. My folks used lamp light and got water and vegetables from the farmer. Daddy worked on the building project, and when his part was done my folks went across Kentucky to another job at Charlestown, Indiana. The powder plant at Charlestown also hired Daddy as a steam fitter. The trailer was parked in another farmer's yard. That is where I was born.

My dad worked for $12 a day and received $24 for Saturday work on those jobs. He was in his 40s at that time.

The next job they went to was in or near Childersburg, Alabama, where Daddy was working when the tragedy happened at Pearl Harbor. One of my mother's nephews, Fred Ray, was on a ship that was blown up; he was presumed dead. His funeral was at Perryville, Missouri, where his parents lived. Sometime later, Fred was miraculously found alive, and he is alive to this very day. A ship had picked him up and taken him to another country.

My folks left the Alabama job and moved to Rohwer, Arkansas, near McGehee. My dad worked in what was known as the Jap Camp — where the Japanese people who were moved out of California were housed during the War. The Japanese could buy the best food at the commissary there, but everyone else had ration stamps.

Because of the War my dad had access to all these jobs. My mom has told me she and my dad found it most interesting. I think they had more than they actually needed, because when I was in high school my dad found one or two of those old uncashed paychecks he'd tucked away and forgotten about.

Jo Ann Miller
Huffman, Texas

Brothers?

A prisoner of war camp was not far from our town during World War II. German soldiers captured in Europe were housed at this camp. Several of them worked on farms in the area, and a few worked for our nearby neighbor. At times they were over at our place. They had a pretty good life and seemed to be enjoying it.

One day several truckloads of the prisoners were taken through town. As they went by they waved at everyone, and people waved at them. But there was a certain amount of mystery about these fellows from so far away who were our enemies, here because they were captured in war.

As they went through town there were a few of us in my uncle's store watching them through the window. Suddenly, one little girl about 10 years old came into the store and said to her dad, "Daddy, I waved at those fellows, was that OK?" He said to her, "Sure, that was all right. I was over there in World War I, and some of them may be your brothers."

Carl W. Franke
Tucson, Arizona

Patriotic Children

Even the children during World War II were aware of being patriotic and helping with the war effort.

I was in the fourth grade in a rural school at the time. The teacher asked us to bring newspapers and crushed tin cans. She would take them to the salvage center in town. She urged us to save our pennies and nickels to buy saving stamps instead of candy. When we had enough stamps saved we could buy a War Bond. How patriotic we felt!

But the oddest things we gathered were ripe, dried milkweed pods with the seeds and the silk in them. The teacher told us that the soft down in the pods was to be used as a filler in clothing and bedding for the solders to make it warm, yet not heavy.

The theater manager sometimes offered tickets to a movie if we would bring two or three pounds of scrap iron to him. Of course, we wanted to see the show, so we hunted for scrap iron on the farm and took it to the manager in exchange for a ticket to see the show. As children, we worked hard, to be patriotic.

JoAnn Fullner
Wisner, Nebraska

Get Your Shootin' Irons Out

When a serviceman was home on leave during World War II, he was supposed to wear his uniform whenever he was out in public. But we had one fellow in our town who was quite an independent character. When he came home on leave after seeing a lot of action in the South Pacific, he was even more independent and aggressive, and he didn't want to wear his uniform at all times.

One time when the town cop saw him in public, he approached the serviceman and told him he had to be wearing his uniform and to go home and get it on. This young man, who had seen and used much bigger guns than anyone in town ever saw, and had seen death at its worst, wasn't easily intimidated. He said to the cop, "OK, get your shootin' irons out and try to make me do it. I'm not wearing my uniform if I don't want to, and if you want to make something of it, get your shootin' irons out and try to make me do so."

Well, the cop was dumfounded. He didn't know what to do, and he wasn't about to take on this young war hero in any kind of fashion he was being invited to. So the cop went to the mayor and told him what had happened and asked the mayor what he should do. The mayor said, "Forget about it; leave him alone."

Carl W. Franke
Tucson, Arizona

A Wondrous Yellow Dot

I was born a year after America entered World War II. Although I was only 3 years old when it ended, my mind still holds a picture of Dad sitting at the kitchen table listening to war news on the radio. Dad's face was troubled, and I remember a tense, worried feeling in the air. Dad's brother, my Uncle Abe, was over there somewhere fighting.

Mother used ration coupons for certain items, and one especially fascinated me. She bought white oleo in a package with a yellow dot. When the dot was pressed, it released color, and she kneaded it until the contents looked as good as butter. The taste I've forgotten, but I remember squeezing the yellow dot.

Uncle Abe came home to thankful, cheering relatives. I held the Purple Heart he showed me, but not long after it became a treasured keepsake. He survived the War, but was killed in a car accident a few weeks after arriving home. He was 24, and my hero.

Judy Barnes
Rathdrum, Idaho

Sneak Attack On Dairy Barn

A German submarine was off the coast of Maine, a mile or two, and the crew was very thirsty. They could see a dance hall all lit up through their field glasses, but otherwise things seemed to be quiet. They went ashore in their small boat, found a dairy in a barn and milked some of the cows. They took what milk they could carry back with them, and they did this for several days before departing.

Howard W. Werry
Orlando, Florida

Promise Fulfilled

It was wartime. My brother was in the service. My father, in his early 60s, could usually cope with the work on his little farm. But when I came home for a brief vacation, I found that my parents had a problem. After having some dental work done, my father was too weak to work outside at all. We worried about him. Had the tooth extraction hurt his heart?

My mother and I tried to fill in for him. Though the chores were light, we were awkward, and unaccustomed to some of the work. Mother milked the one cow; I did other chores. We rigged a crude cable between the corn crib and feed floor to make it easier to carry corn to the pigs.

One morning, we pulled a promise card from our little Scripture promise box and read: "Call upon me, and I will answer thee, and show thee great and mighty things which thou knowest not." We took Dad to the doctor that day, where we received good news. Though the dental work had been a strain on Dad, the doctor assured us that he would recover from it.

Much relieved, we returned home. Then we remarked that if we could just get a hired man for a few days, all would be well. But Dad said, "That is impossible. This is wartime. No men are available."

Almost at that very instant, we saw my soldier brother walking into our yard. We rushed to welcome him. He told us that his superior officer had offered the furlough. How good it was to have his company and his help. It seemed that the doctor's good news and my brother's unexpected furlough were among the "great and mighty things" of the promise card.

Gwen McKinley
Traer, Iowa

Nylons — A Real Treasure

During World War II there was a shortage of hose. I remember one old friend guarding her one good pair, keeping them in a fruit jar with the lid on tight. She wore them only on good weather Sundays and to funerals.

One Saturday while uptown, I noticed a long line, even out to the sidewalk, at Murphys. I investigated and found a shipment of hose had just come in. They had moved the boxes to the back of the store and were selling them from there, only one pair per person. I bought mine, then went to the end of the line and bought a pair for my mother. I went again for a pair for my sister. Now as I observe the well-stocked nylon shelves and read their expensive ads, I think of that time when one good pair of nylons was really a treasure.

Florence Palmer
Marshall, Illinois

Prisoners Share Culture

I was a young child of 4 or 5 when World War II began. My daddy quit teaching and went to work at Fort Leonard Wood, Missouri. He moved the family, which consisted of him, my mother, my younger brother and me to Fort Leonard Wood.

There was a German prison camp at Fort Leonard Wood. My daddy worked inside the prison camp for a while. The prisoners did jobs around the post. I still have a jewelry box that they made for my mother. I also have a metal dustpan that was made by one of the prisoners.

During those war years, even though I was very young, I learned about different races and cultures. I often wonder what happened to many of those people.

Loma Jean (Wood) Lawler
Strafford, Missouri

Shrinking Violet

During World War II, I was in my teens. Army trains went through our small town and stopped for a moment; the soldier boys opened windows, sometimes coming to the platforms between cars to throw out slips of paper with their names and addresses, hoping we would write.

We knew a train was coming on a certain date, so I bought a pretty but inexpensive crepe dress. My friend's father took us to meet the train.

As we waited, there was a sudden shower. We ran for the station, but it was closed. As we went back, I found my new dress had shrunk to well above my knees, clinging like wallpaper. There were also ugly spots of dye on my slip. No soldier boy was going to see me that way, so I hid in the car. Next time we met a train, I took no chances, but wore an old, well-laundered dress.

Violet Beard
Marshall, Illinois

106

New York City After Italy's Surrender

A highlight memory for me of World War II happened during my vacation time in 1943. My friend Clara and I scheduled our vacation time together from our different office jobs. Clara was to visit her boyfriend who was in the Navy and stationed in New York City. His sister, Mary, was living in the city and had an apartment where we stayed during our visit.

The start of our vacation trip was a train from Kansas City's Union Station to Chicago. It pulled out about 10 p.m. that Friday evening. We got in Chicago early Saturday morning and had a little time to sightsee before our next train. On Sunday morning, we saw the Hudson River, had a glimpse of West Point, then on into the New York City station.

One day we went out for breakfast and then on our walking tour. Coming out from a shop, we saw a lot of confetti on the streets. Asking about it, we heard the grand and welcome news of Italy's surrender. From the windows of the upper floors of the buildings, the workers were throwing down confetti, toilet paper, scraps of new material, etc. onto the sidewalk below. It collected in great heaps and was being kicked and scattered about on the streets. There were so much beautiful material that I just had to pick up as much of the prettier scraps of new velvet, printed jersey and crepe as I could stuff in the paper bags I had.

The crowd was very large; it seemed all the people from all the stores poured out on the streets. Surely it couldn't have been better on New Year's Eve.

After the trip was over, I went to spend the rest of my vacation with my parents down on the farm. I took the scrap material with me, and my mother was as thrilled as I had been when picking it up. Later on, Mom made two kimonos by stitching many of the beautiful pieces together in crazy-quilt fashion, adding varied fancy embroidery stitches around each different scrap. Each kimono was lovely and a special memento of Italy's surrender.

Esther Lewis
Mission, Kansas

Where There's A Will...

During the second World War, my family and relatives were farmers, living in northern Grant County, Oklahoma. Farmers in this area were basically self-sufficient in regards to food, meat, vegetables and fruit. Car tires were our main concern.

For several weeks, Mother had kept mentioning to Dad about the condition of the tires on the car. Dad's view on most anything was that if there was farm work that needed to be done, everything else was secondary.

With the attack on Pearl Harbor, she made one last effort to activate him. But as usual, something else needed to be done. He finally got to the service station the day after tire sales were restricted. Consequently, we went through four years of almost-bald tires on the car.

For a farmer such as my dad, gasoline was not too much of a problem. Each vehicle or tractor had its own ration book, and you were supposed to store the gas for each in separate tanks. The Ration Board did selective inspections. One neighbor had only one tank, so he solved this dilemma with two faucets. He took gas for the big truck from the big faucet and gas for the pick-up from the little faucet.

The local joke was that the inspector could tell if you were using tractor gas in your car. All he had to do was take the cap off the tank, and if it was black inside, you were using tractor gas.

Our landlord had an old Model T Ford that used very little gas. He would drive to town and fill up the tank, then when he got home, he would drain the gas into glass jugs. These he would store away for use in case my dad ran short of farm gas. The next day he would repeat the operation until all of his coupons were used up.

When sugar rationing came along, each family had to register for ration coupons. In doing so, you had to swear on oath that you had only a predetermined limited amount of sugar on hand. My mother, like many other women, had been storing extra sugar prior to the rationing. She took her surplus sugar, added water, and cooked it into a syrup, which she then sealed in fruit jars. She could then truthfully say she had no surplus sugar on hand. As it worked out, we had plenty of sugar even with rationing. At the end of the war, she still had some sugar syrup on hand.

Ivan L. Pfalser
Caney, Kansas

Students Did What They Could

An ominous air lingered over our country when I entered high school in 1941 as a green freshman just out of country school. Fighting in Europe had gone on for two years, and we wondered if and when we would be drawn into the War. Our chosen radio program on the afternoon of December 7 was interrupted with the news that the Japs had bombed Pearl Harbor! We were at war!

Life for the next four years was to be radically different than what I had anticipated. We were deprived of many things because of shortages, especially the gas shortage, but our patriotism and our feeling of doing something toward the war effort made up for it.

One by one, male teachers were drafted or enlisted, until we had only three older men teachers. Women took their places, but it was impossible to find a football coach. Our superintendent became the official coach, while a young man who worked at the post office was the acting coach. He led our team to victory after victory.

One of our class members left school in his junior year to enlist in the Army. He was killed in action, and we attended his funeral shortly before our graduation.

We had no field trips, no annual; our music and sports contests were held at schools close by. We got on the Greyhound bus downtown to go shopping in other towns. But we survived. What a feeling of ecstasy when V-E Day was proclaimed in May and V-J Day in August of 1945. We could start to get back to normal.

Jeanette Larson
Story City, Iowa

109

Washington, D.C., During The War

One day a representative of the FBI came to our little town, looking for girls interested in working for the FBI in Washington, D.C. I was asked by our local town police officer if I'd be interested in this opportunity. Listening to the FBI man tell of the employment, wages and a chance to help in the war effort, I knew this was what I wanted to do. I was fingerprinted, investigated and cleared for FBI employment.

Working for the FBI, I was trained to be a fingerprint classifier. We were to help classify the huge stacks of fingerprints of military and defense workers. There were rooms filled with fingerprint cards waiting to be classified.

The FBI building was heavily guarded, and we could only enter by showing our identification pins. All government buildings were guarded.

The streets of Washington were crowded on weekends with servicemen from nearby training bases. The men were lonely and passing time by seeing the nation's capital.

Most government buildings did allow servicemen to tour the building during set hours. Government workers like us could only tour these buildings when accompanied by a serviceman. We would ask a serviceman standing on the street to take the tour with us. After the tour, we often found a doughnut shop where we would talk more, before leaving the serviceman to continue his lonesome day.

Myrtle May Duin
George, Iowa

Eyes On The Skies

I was a young fellow, just 30, married with one daughter when the war got close enough for us to jump in. I was lucky to have a job making $50 a week, working for my father-in-law. We operated a small factory making photo supplies for Macys, Gimbles and Wannamakers.

Right after Pearl Harbor, I was standing just outside the big iron fence that ran all around our property, talking to my father-in-law. I thought that Hitler would be landing on our shores any day.

It wasn't but a month after that a man came to our little town representing the Air Force. Somehow he got hold of me. He wanted us to build a spotter's post near town and man it 24 hours a day. We were to spot and report all aircraft in the sky. In those days there weren't many airplanes flying anyway, but the whole country was running scared. I got picked for the job, which paid nothing, because I was handy and anxious to help keep Hitler from our shores.

Our little village of Unionville, New York, was situated in the southeastern part of the state. My first problem was where to get the material to build a spotter's post. I finally saw a bunch of storm windows leaning against the old Baptist church. This was no longer a church, but was being used as a community house.

I asked the mayor if they would mind if we used those windows to build our little building, and it was OK with the village. I had a trailer I made out of an old Model T frame, and I pulled it behind my '37 Chevy. Two friends and I loaded these windows on the trailer and hauled them about a mile out of town. We had picked a site on the top of the highest hill we could find. With those windows we assembled a glass-roofed building big enough for three people to sit in. I hauled up a good supply of coal donated by one of the local creameries for the little potbellied stove in the rear. Next, I called the telephone company and ordered a telephone installed, as we had to call in every aircraft we saw to White Plains, New York. We had to give the estimated speed, direction and type of aircraft, if we could tell. I had the telephone installed, then asked the town fathers to pay up. They refused but soon paid the bill.

It was the early part of February, and it was almost zero outside. Fred Gilson, Herald Paugh and I were on duty from midnight until 4 a.m. As we looked out of our glass house, the stars seemed so close we could touch them. We could see for miles. About 10 miles away as the crow flies, we could see High Point Monument.

This monument is on the highest point in the state of New Jersey. After sitting there a little while, we noticed the red light on top of the monument kept blinking on and off. Fred said, "I bet they are sending some kind of secret code." After that we watched it more carefully, and sure enough, it looked like Morse code to us.

Harold reminded us that we were not that far from the coast; maybe they were sending a message to a submarine in the Atlantic Ocean. We thought it would be just like those darn Germans. We got real worked up over that light blinking on and off. Sometimes it would blink three times, pause, then two times, then five times in a row. Finally I reached for the telephone book and looked up the number for High Point. We were going to get to the bottom of this. I dialed the number, and it rang and rang and rang. It was after 2 a.m., but finally someone answered. The voice on the other end had a German accent, or so we thought. Right then, any accent would have been German to us. We tried to tell him about the messages being sent out, but we just couldn't get through to him what we wanted to tell him. I hung up, and about 3 a.m. we called again. The same fellow answered, and this time we just couldn't get him to understand. We tried two more times with no success, so we finally settled down to the idea that maybe it was a short circuit that the wind helped along.

This spotter's post was used for several years, and as the war wound down, the post was moved into town in back of the school. I guess it served its purpose well.

Howard W. Werry
Orlando, Florida

Doing Without Just Part Of Doing Duty

I still have my last ration book issued in 1943, and it still has some stamps in it. On the back it says, "Never buy rationed goods without ration stamps, never pay more than the legal price."

A lot of things were rationed, such as gas, tires, shoes, coffee, meat and sugar. The one I remember most is sugar. I was going to high school, and I boarded in town. Sometimes extra sugar stamps were issued, and my mother would instruct me to go to the courthouse and stand in line for the extra stamps. Recipes that used very little sugar or honey were in great demand. Some things were not rationed, they just were not available. Our clock quit, and the only timepiece we had was my grandfather's pocket watch.

When things are hard to get, the black market flourishes. Dan, who had married a local girl, was from the city. He brought back hard-to-get things and sold them for highly elevated prices. We were married in 1946, and it was the custom to give candy bars at the shivaree. Candy bars were not available in our small town, so my husband ordered from Dan. Sure enough, he came through with enough Baby Ruths and Butterfingers to treat the crowd.

Sheets could not be bought either, and when I received one from my mother-in-law and one from a neighbor at my shower, I was very happy to have enough bedding for our one bed.

One shortage I had never heard about until January 16, 1944, was the bubblegum shortage. Our pastor told the story about not being able to buy bubblegum, so one boy whose dad had access to the PX was able to to get some. Pastor said he was number 19 on the list, and by the time the gum got to him it was no longer pink and had no taste to it, but he said he couldn't imagine how it was by the time it got to number 30 on the list. Most people made the best of it; after all, if our fighting men needed assistance it was our duty to help the war effort.

Marie Holzwarth
St. Francis, Kansas

Prisoners Provide Labor

During World War II, we had ration books for tires, shoes, sugar, coffee and gasoline. We lived on the farm and raised sugar beets, so we received 100 pounds of sugar a year. My husband was a "sugaroholic" and never learned to use less. When we exchanged work on the farm, the neighbors just didn't put it on the table. He always covered his oatmeal with a layer of brown sugar and put several teaspoons of sugar in his tea and coffee.

Since we lived on an irrigated farm, we raised sugar beets and potatoes; both required lots of hand labor. We used German prisoners of war to hoe the beets and pick up the potatoes. When they came in the mornings they brought a thick milk soup for their lunch. When we harvested the potatoes I cooked maybe a bucket of small ones, then put butter on them and browned them in the oven. They liked those, but they wouldn't eat sweet corn — that was pig food.

In the summer the prisoners ate their lunch in our yard under the trees. One day I showed them a *Life* magazine that had lots of pictures. On the front was a picture of one's hometown, and he could see his parents' house, so he knew they were OK. One of them was a pianist, and he loved to come in and play the piano. The others enjoyed the music too.

My husband and his family had lived in the same town as the superintendent of the prison camp, and he invited our family to the camp to eat Thanksgiving Day dinner with him and his family. We sat on the wooden benches and had the same food as the prisoners. My boys, ages 6 and 8, were impressed. What I remember most was the big silver bowl of fruit.

Frances Hoyt Trail
McCook, Nebraska

No Heil Here

I recall school in wartime days. We always said the Pledge of Allegiance every morning. We would say, "I pledge allegiance" and extend our arms straight out toward the flag and hold it, then repeat the rest of the pledge.

This was discontinued because it was considered similar to Hitler's "heil" in Germany.

Mary L. Schofield
Lenox, Iowa

Dressing In The Dark

Here is a humorous story from former neighbors about World War II. They both worked in the shipyards; she on the day shift, he on the late-night shift. They lived in a very small one-bedroom kitchenette apartment. The only entrance was the screened service porch.

One night the husband quietly got out of bed at 11 p.m., dressing in the dark so as not to wake his wife. He walked toward the rear door while putting on his heavy jacket against the cold, slipping his last arm into the jacket as he ducked under the small clothesline strung across the service porch. He quickly walked to the trolley-line stop, arriving just as the trolley arrived.

He walked toward the rear of the trolley, where he saw an empty seat. When he was seated, he saw other passengers he had passed were smiling. He smiled back, wondering what the humor could be at that late hour. Arriving at the shipyard, he went to his work area, and noticed after passing other workers that they were smiling, too.

He removed his jacket and found the answer to the smiles on the faces of people he had passed. When slipping on his jacket in the dark, he did not see his wife's nylons on the small clothesline. The nylons were hanging from the collar down the back of his jacket, bringing smiles to everyone he passed.

His wife had a hearty laugh when he told her, but she almost repeated the incident at a later date. She arose early one morning in the cold pre-dawn darkness, quickly dressed, and hurried to the trolley stop. No one looked at her with laughter. But on arriving at the shipyard office where she worked, she removed her coat, gasped, and quickly put her coat on again.

She had on her shoes, slip, and blouse, but had forgotten to put on her skirt. She quickly caught the next trolley home to finish dressing.

Lucile Hebert
Yucaipa, California

Aunt Lena's Own Victory Garden

My Aunt Lena Berkheimer shared her memories of World War
II with me. She and her husband and two sons lived north of
town. When the government sent Mr. Peterson to urge people to
plant vegetables in their gardens — especially navy beans for the
war effort — she got really put out with his tirade and told him to
go on down the road.

She had plenty to do already, planting a big garden every year
and canning vegetables. One-third of the plot went to asparagus,
which she shared with me and neighbors.

Dorothy Carmann
Riverdale, Nebraska

Keeping The Railroads Going

In 1942, my dad and I were sawing railroad ties for the government, 10 miles south of Macomb, Illinois. We were in a
1,000-acre timber lot. We had seven men working for us, two log
cutters, one log hauler and two men with Dad and me at the mill.
There were two men trimming ties with bark left on them after
going through the mill. We were sawing 100 ties a day, as well as
the lumber off of them. We sawed a little over 14,000 ties in seven
months. I had just turned 38 and was exempt from the Army.

Ernest Danielson
West Burlington, Iowa

I Remember The War

I remember the war years of the early '40s and the honor roll
that stood proudly downtown with all of our boys fighting the big
war. I remember the sign on the window of the door to my father's
two-door grease room, garishly showing the pictures of Hitler,
Mussolini and Tojo with a big "X" over all three, meaning "get rid
of them."

Dad had a gas station, and the farmers and truckers gave him their extra ration stamps, as well as the ones they needed to cover their own needs. The stamps were pasted on big sheets of paper from the board in Dixon. I used to help put the stamps in place. The extra stamps were held for the boys home on leave so they could visit friends and take their girls out.

My father was like a family member to most of the young men home on furlough. In the office of the station, he had a closet door covered with post cards from all over the world that the fighting men of our town had sent. When a soldier boy hit town for a few days, the first place he seemed to go was my dad's. I remember lying awake at night with one or two of the soldiers sitting on the couch just outside my bedroom door. I listened with great interest to the tales they told of what they had seen and done.

When I was in seventh grade, our teacher retired; her man was home from the war. The new teacher who greeted us right after Thanksgiving was a man — our first male teacher in grade school. He is still part of my class reunion. He had been a machine gunner in the South Pacific. He had taken one in the knee and was just out of the hospital at Great Lakes. He had lost a sister in the Philippine Islands when MacArthur left. She was a nurse and had not been heard from since. He needed to get a lot out of his system about the war. We heard it all; no matter what he taught, it ended up in stories of the war. It was the best education anyone could have.

He had a lingo we had to learn. When he told us to do something "on the double" or to "go to the head," at first we just looked at him. That Christmas while shopping with my aunt, I found two books on the leathernecks with vocabulary lists in them. When school started in January, I knew what he was talking about.

After the war when the men came home, they wanted to form a VFW Club. They met for several months in my father's filling station grease room. They brought card tables from home and folding chairs so they could play cards and drink beer.

Grandma Hazel learned to crochet, and made afghans for the veterans at Hines V.A. Hospital. When she had several made, her daughter, my Aunt Hazel, would take her in to the hospital to give them to the men personally. One I remember in particular went to Jim. A happy-go-lucky guy, he was paralyzed from the neck down. He was thrilled with his, for it was made with his high school colors — black and red. He was the center of activities for the other guys at the hospital. He planned trips to ball games, ice shows, etc. Everyone looked up to him. Grandma made him a second afghan when the first was stolen from his wheelchair, which sat just outside his room.

I remember sitting at my grandfather's knee night after night, listening to the big radio as he followed the march of the enemies. Later, I remember when Poland was taken. He said we would soon be in it too. He was right. I grew up listening to the 8 o'clock news on WBBM, eating breakfast and cheering as each mile was taken, closer and closer to the Rhine. I followed it on Uncle Wilbur's big map pinned up in the den, hearing of places I had never heard of before.

I remember the day the War ended in the Pacific. Lots of kids had firecrackers and caps left from the Fourth of July. I took my uncle's hammer, and laying a whole roll of caps on the sidewalk, hit roll after roll. There was laughter and tears. It was over at last. We hugged each other.

Crescence Stadeble
DeKalb, Illinois

Paint Your Nylons On And Draw The Seams

Several years ago, following the death of my parents, I was going through their possessions and found a number of various kinds of ration books from World War II. That brought back memories of what things were like in those days. I was a high school student then. Gas was one of the things that was rationed, and a family was happy to get three gallons a week with an "A" stamp to get around town. No long family trips.

My parents were farmers, so we were allowed more gas than city or town people. Another item that was in short supply was tires, but farmers were encouraged to raise all the crops they could, so it was easier for them to get tires, too.

For people in town, a substitute for butter called margarine was available. At that time it wasn't very desirable, as it was white in color and resembled lard. A couple of brands came with a little packet of yellow coloring enclosed, which you had to mix into the margarine yourself. At least by doing that it looked as if it would taste better.

Another thing that was almost impossible to buy was nylon hosiery. One manufacturer even came out with a thick tan liquid with an applicator — you could paint your legs to look as if you had nylons on. They even included a pen so you could draw on a seam down the back of your leg. When the War ended and nylon wasn't needed so much for parachutes, I was working in a department store. I can remember the long lines of women waiting to buy nylons when they became available again.

I can't recall anyone complaining. In those days everyone was very patriotic and willing to do without if it was necessary to win the War. I wonder if that would be the same today?

Elinor Jensen
Wayne, Nebraska

V For Victory In The Yard

1943 found me 10 years old, living with my parents, six brothers and sisters, and one married brother in a huge farmhouse in rural southwest Iowa. An impressive *Gone With the Wind* type stairway afforded us many a ride, so the banister was never dusty. Upstairs, the builder must have economized, because two bedrooms, two hallways and three closets were never painted.

In those World War II paper-rationing days, if we could find a pencil, we kids would draw and write all over those walls as high up as we could reach. Then we would stand on a chair and continue to the ceiling.

Ours was a very happy, big, boisterous, fun-loving family during this time, marred only by the second World War. Two married sisters had husbands in the service. One came back to our home to wait out her husband's overseas duty in the Aleutian Islands. They had sold their grocery store upon receiving his draft notice. After a sale of the groceries, everything that didn't sell was stored in one of the big closets in our 18-room farmhouse. It was sugar rationing time, and my siblings and I discovered cough drops stored there. They tasted as good as candy.

My sister waited out the birth of their first child alone. She suffered pregnancy complications — some type of itching all over her body. Mom and Dad would hear her pacing the floor many nights over this terrible itching. At last their baby girl was born. One day this tiny girl was asleep on the bed my sister and I shared. Mom and my sister heard a terrible noise. Rushing in, they found the baby asleep; the ceiling plaster had fallen and just missed the baby.

Brother Dale followed the War battles through our daily paper. Each afternoon we'd get off the school bus and race up our long lane to the house. He usually was first because he wanted to get the newspaper first. He would explain about the various battles and where the Allies were, using the photos in the Des Moines, Iowa, *Tribune*.

Dale was very patriotic. His job was to mow our farmyard with a reel lawn mower. He would leave an unmown "V" for victory in the middle of the yard for traffic to see. We were so proud of him.

Mary L. Schofield
Lenox, Iowa

Smiles For A Stranger

In the early '40s, my parents moved from their farm to Kansas City, Kansas, 120 miles away.

We often made weekend trips back to our hometown for holiday dinners and short visits. It was a common sight to see a soldier hitchhiking to get home or back to camp. My Dad never passed one by. We enjoyed meeting all the young men, learning where they were stationed and about their homes and families. We felt the gesture was our patriotic duty and looked forward to it.

As soon as they stowed their baggage and settled in, introductions were made. My brother and I, early grade schoolers, sat spellbound in the back seat listening intently to the conversations up front. We strained our ears as Daddy said, "Hi, where you going?" The polite soldiers were regarded by the two of us as heroes.

One severely cold night, a hitchhiking soldier soon fell into a deep sleep, his head falling over on my mother's shoulder. She dared not move and awaken him, affording him the chance to rest. My brother and I remained unusually quiet as he slept. When Daddy reached our corner to turn off the highway, we were approximately 50 miles from the soldier's destination, Camp Crowder, near Neosho, Missouri. Daddy pulled the car to a stop and regrettably woke our passenger. "I'm sorry, we'll have to let you out here." Sadly, we drove away, leaving him beside the road hoping to catch another ride soon.

There was no reason to fear a stranger or hesitate to offer a helping hand. I can still see a man in uniform grab his duffel bag and hurry to the car as Daddy pulled over onto the shoulder. A smiling young man climbed in and said, "Hi, sure nice of you folks to give me a lift." We all smiled back at our new friend.

Janice I. Kinman
Carthage, Missouri

Noises In The Night

We were quite young when the War was over. I was only about 10, but the sound of many planes is still an ominous one to me.

The Iowa plains were one route the bombers flew over to cross the continent, and often I was awakened in the night by their thunderous sound. I remember asking my cousins whether they had heard the noises in the night. They assured me that they had, and that those were fighter planes on their way to the front.

Barbara Queen
Rosemead, California

Doctor Shortage

There is always a doctor shortage in rural areas. After the War started, we lost almost all our M.D.s, with only one other physician that the Army did not call into service.

I needed brace repairs. I was sent to a hospital in St. Louis, after the head doctor at the state hospital where I had been treated after polio went to Europe.

My sis had her baby at our house when she did not make it to the nearest hospital 30 miles away. Our small rural hospital had closed when its only doctor was called by the Army. She had no doctor until after the birth.

Jewell Cooper
Bolivar, Missouri

College Scrap-Metal Drive

During the War years of 1942-44, I was a college student at the Central University of Iowa, there to obtain an elementary teaching degree.

As girls stood in line near dormitory mailboxes, there were often shouts of joy, intimate smiles and heart-breaking tears. We waited patiently, and prayed for any kind of a letter, note, post card or picture from our classmates, boyfriends and brothers who were serving in the U.S. military forces far away.

There was much excitement when a weekend leave was permitted. There was also great disappointment when shipping-out orders were announced, many times to an unknown destination. We said fond farewells, never knowing where, when, or if we would be together again.

One day our college classes were dismissed for a citywide scrap-metal drive in Pella, Iowa. There were not many young men left in college; they had enlisted or been drafted for active military service.

I was one of the droves of girls who walked the city streets, knocking on every door asking for any scrap metal.

We collected such things as old kitchen utensils, clocks, pans, skillets, tools, irons, buckets, toasters, coffeepots, waffle makers and even children's toys!

We met trucks at some of the intersections in Pella and deposited whatever we had been given. Toward the end of that day, the trucks dumped their load of various metals all in one scrap-pile near the railroad tracks. There it could soon be re-loaded into a railroad car to start the journey to be transformed into more useful war materials.

As a loyal group of C.U. I. students, we girls gathered 'round that ugly pile of old metal and gave thanks to God. We asked him to please "bless these bits," and speed them on their way — to help bring for everyone a future, a better day.

Hope C. Robinson
Yale, Iowa

Traveling Refrigerator

Since my husband was a farmer, he was exempt from serving in the Armed Forces in World War II, but we were affected by the War in many ways. There was a scarcity of many products and rationing of many necessities.

My brother-in-law who was in the Armed Forces was sent to Australia. His wife moved into an apartment in the city and stored their furniture. Since it was considered necessary that a refrigerator be used constantly, theirs was sent to us to use. That was a big help. We had no refrigerator, and had been hanging perishable food down in a well or keeping it in the cellar. The government packed and shipped the refrigerator to us. Because of the scarcity of such items, we carefully saved the lumber used in the shipping crate, and we also saved all the nails.

Tires were rationed and in very short supply. The government ordered that we drive at a slow speed to keep from having "blow-outs," which could cause serious accidents. I remember driving to town with my small son. He was watching the speedometer and said, "Mommy, slow down! You are going 40 miles an hour!"

Metal was almost nonexistent. For Christmas, my son received a toy wagon made completely of wood. He also got a sled that was all wood, no metal — even on the runners. At a later time, my husband fastened strips of iron on the runners, to make them more efficient. Almost 50 years later, that wooden sled is still hanging in a storage shed on our farm.

When the War was over, our brother-in-law came home. He took his refrigerator, but we were able to buy one of our own.

Hazel Millenbruch
Home, Kansas

Everyone Had A Part

Both of my parents were too old to go in World War II. They lived in Liberal, Kansas. My dad helped farmers and worked for the Highway Department. My mother cleaned houses and babysat for women who went to work. Many of the men were in the Army. My husband farmed.

Gas and tires were rationed. All windshields had the sticker, "Is this trip necessary?" Shoes were also rationed. We bought our children shoes that were made of a paper product. When they got wet, they fell apart. We used our coupons to buy them some more. We received tokens for change.

We traded our coffee stamps to friends for sugar stamps. We didn't use coffee. We were only allowed so many stamps at a time. Our third child was on Pet Milk formula. We were only allowed so much, but my dad knew a grocer, and he would buy us some. Two nieces worked in a grocery store, and they saved some so we always had milk for the baby.

The government built a new air base in Liberal to train pilots to fly the 224 bombers. My dad got a job at the air base as a fireman. If a plane got into trouble landing, they were there with foam and water to put it out if it caught fire. There were many crashes. Many of the boys who were training had never been near a plane.

One Thanksgiving the family was at our house for dinner. Just as I glanced out the window, there was a big noise and a huge explosion. Two planes had collided in mid-air just north of Liberal. Later we drove down to see it. All the crew members of both planes had been killed.

Near Moscow, Kansas, another plane crashed. The pilot couldn't get out, and people couldn't get close enough to help him. They just had to stand and watch it burn.

Everyone in one way or another had a part in the War. Long days were spent in the fields to produce food. We made do with what we had.

Liberal was a small town, and the housing shortage was terrible. People lived in chicken houses. It is too bad that some people took advantage and charged terrible rent. Finally the government passed a rent control program.

It was a happy day when the War was over.

Daisy Scott
Hugoton, Kansas

Extending A Green Thumb

During the second World War, things were hard on the home front, too. Besides having to cope with rationing and shortages, the women who were at home were faced with the task of growing their own food.

Since my mother was a leader in 4-H Clubs as well as Home Extension Clubs, she had close contact with the county Extension office.

The county in which we lived had a project going called a Victory Garden. This required a respected leader of the community to go from place to place in her neighborhood and give advice on "How to Successfully Produce Food For the Family."

Mother's task was to share with the neighbors exactly how to water their garden to conserve water and still produce a crop of vegetables. We planted rows one and two close together, leaving a little wider space, then planting rows three and four close together. This system was carried out until the plot was planted. Between the rows planted close together, a ditch was dug, and water was allowed to flow down these ditches to the end of the row.

Our garden produced enough for my mother — with the help of my sister and me — to can vegetables for the entire year, saving the store-bought canned foods for the boys serving in the Armed Forces.

Delores Utecht
Wayne, Nebraska

Unrealistic Regulations

Many things were rationed in World War II, including sugar. But if a person had fruit to can, there was a special provision for canning sugar. A friend of mine had an abundance of pears. This friend told me: "If you can get sugar for them, I will give you a bushel of pears." I went to the Ration Board to apply for sugar. I was told, "After you get the pears, come and apply." I told my friend, who said, "I will give them after I know you have the sugar." So I had nothing.

Mary Gardener
Forest Park, Illinois

Housing Shortage

My husband and I were married when he returned on furlough in March 1943. I finished my fourth year of teaching and left by train for Savannah, Georgia, in May.

It was very difficult to find an apartment, and his pay as a private in the Air Force wasn't much. I had saved some money, but our first apartment was one small, filthy room with a bed and dresser uptown on Lincoln Street. We bought a cabinet, a three-burner kerosene stove, a small table and two chairs and started house-keeping.

We had a wooden tub and a washboard, and I could go out the window onto the roof of the two-story building to hang my clothes. Our room was on the third floor. We soon discovered bed bugs. Soldiers and sailors came and went, and we knew about the woman across the hall.

Most of the time the halls were dark at night, and sometimes there were no bulbs in the bathroom, which was quite a distance down the hall. I would not open our door until I heard my husband's voice, and I would not go to the bathroom after dark alone. My husband knew the place would be raided, and we desperately tried to find another apartment.

We watched the papers. Finally, when he had a day off, we started down the streets; he on one side, I on the other. We knocked on doors and asked, "Do you know where we can find an apartment?" After we had walked all day, we asked a lady who was sitting on the porch. She answered, "Why yes, I think you can get one right here." It was a private home with three apartments, and praise God, we had asked on the right day — a couple was moving out.

The apartment was probably 12-by-15 feet, with a bedroom at one end and a kitchen at the other, all furnished. It even had a lavatory in the kitchen, and the bath was just down the hall. It was like heaven after living in that dump for two months. We feared asking how much, because we knew it would be beyond our reach, but we were amazed at the price — $4 a week. I asked, "Are there bed bugs here?" She answered, "No, and don't you bring any!"

We sold our little dab of furniture and packed our kitchen supplies and clothes after carefully searching for bed bugs. We lived in that one room about three years.

Marvin was an M.P. and had some exciting experiences. One night as he guarded the gate, a captain and a major crawled under the fence as they were returning to base. One said to the other, "Well, we made it!" Marvin approached and exclaimed, "Not quite!" And of course, he reported them.

Mrs. Marvin L. Tate
Abilene, Kansas

Narrow Escape In Plant Disaster

I had a narrow escape after my husband, Louis, went overseas and I came back to Nebraska. I went to work at the Carnusher Ammunition Plant, putting boosters in the big bombs.

I had worked there several months when I was transferred to driving a donkey (Ford tractor hauling ammo). This particular day I was coming down the ramp, walking with the maintenance man. I got my donkey and stopped in the building where they were filling the bombs to see if they needed any more TNT. I talked to Shorty and the foreman, then went on to the next building.

I had just gotten to the next building when the one I was just in blew up. Nobody ever knew what caused the accident. Everyone was killed, and they never did find enough parts of the maintenance man or foreman to identify them.

When we heard the explosion, everyone tore outside. The racks and cement were coming down around us. My first thought was, "This is what Louis is going through in Germany." A truck came and picked us up to take us to the change house — it was a mess, and our clothes were, too. They took us to the cafeteria, and everything there was a mess, too. One of the girls who rode out with us every day was killed.

I feel I certainly had an angel on my side. When I went back later to get my belongings, they told me my donkey was still in the doorway, and my sweatshirt was on it.

Dorothy Drake
Arcadia, Nebraska

Thoroughly American

We were of German extraction, our grandparents having come over to Iowa from Germany. We young grandchildren didn't speak any language other than English. Nor did most of the wives of my father's brothers. We all felt thoroughly American, and there was no question about where our loyalties were during the war, but my father warned my mother to keep her visits to town for groceries as few and brief as possible.

"Don't stay around and talk to people, just go in, do your business and get right home," he'd say.

She didn't really seem to believe that anything would happen, but Daddy quit his Saturday night visits to town and stayed at home on the farm. Nobody wanted anything to happen, and no one was taking any chances.

Barbara Queen
Rosemead, California

Most Practical Choice

It was the spring of 1944, and we had been married only a month or two. I was in need of a new pair of shoes, so I walked downtown and came home with a pair of high heels. White, toeless, with a perky little bow and just a strap around the back. I used my shoe stamp that was to last me 'til the new stamp, which I think was for six months.

I was 17, just a kid, and they were my first high heels. When my husband, a practical farm boy, came home and saw me wobbling around in them, he was anything but happy with my choice.

It's been almost 50 years, but I can still see those shoes as if it were yesterday.

Elsie R. Hinote
Kansas City, Kansas

Ice Cream Without Sugar

When the news of Pearl Harbor came over the radio that Sunday afternoon in December, my husband, Leonard Bird, was teaching vocational agriculture in Norton (Kansas) High School.

In a couple of weeks, they took all the young faculty men off to service. The only men left were a music teacher who had only one hand, school principal Mr. Travis and my husband. My husband coached football and wrestling, plus his regular duties, and they filled in with all women teachers.

The faculty wives changed the card parties to sewing for the Red Cross, helping some of the wives whose husbands were gone.

I can remember meat rationing. I raised a big flock of chickens and sold them; three-pound chicken for $1.25, more if I dressed them. I couldn't fill all my orders that came in.

Sugar was also rationed, but that wasn't so hard. We made our good old homemade ice cream with white syrup and extra vanilla.

Emilie Bird
Beatrice, Nebraska

My Favorite Sugar Rationing Cake
1. Sift together
    2 cups flour
    1 package pudding (non-instant)
    1/4 teaspoon salt
    1 rounded teaspoon baking powder
    1 teaspoon soda
    2 teaspoons cocoa (optional)
2. Beat together
    1/2 cup shortening
    1 cup syrup
3. Beat 1 egg, add 1 cup sour milk
4. Add dry ingredients. Beat well. Bake at 350 degrees for about 30 minutes.

Hazel Wilson
Mountain View, California

Nylons Recycled By Pastor's Wife
Nylon hose were very precious items. Our pastor's wife, who in later years became my mother-in-law, had the knack for repairing runs in nylons. She had a hooked instrument, similar to a very fine crochet hook. With this, she would start at the base of the run and

weave the loose thread between the cross threads back up to the top of the run. She did such meticulous work, one could not detect there ever was a run. Needless to say, she kept busy mending nylons for church members and friends.

Our pastor conducted German-speaking services once a month. After the War broke out, congregation members opted to discontinue these services. Because of the animosity caused by the War, they feared destruction of church property by patriotic citizens.

My husband's uncle owned and operated a filling station at the time. The family suspicioned he was selling black market tires because he seemed to be increasing his bank roll. This was never proven.

Betty Wittig
Wayne, Nebraska

Balloon Bomb In Missouri

Sometime late in World War II, probably in January 1945, I was living in Bolivar, Missouri. I got up late one night to check the fire in a big coal stove. It was very cold outside, probably around zero. A light snow was being carried on the northwest wind.

As I went through the dark room, I saw a flash of light through a southwest window. I thought to myself, "That's funny, I've seen lightning in a snowstorm before, but never when it was so cold."

I never thought any more about it, even the next day when Dad, who had been staying out at the farm some distance west of town, came in with a story about an explosion he had seen and heard to the south the night before. He swore it was a bomb.

I thought, "Why would anybody waste a bomb on a frozen Missouri cow pasture?" There was no sound of planes, though, and nothing more was said about it, not even when stories came around about remnants of a Japanese balloon being found farther east.

It wasn't until after the War, when I was reading about the Japanese launching balloons carrying bombs over the United States, that it dawned on me that I had seen one exploding.

Since there was no report of damage, the bomb probably exploded in the air, and the wind carried the balloon farther to the southeast.

It's sort of amusing to think — some farmer may have been shaken out of his bed if that thing went off over his house in the middle of the night.

V. E. Carter
Topeka, Kansas

—■—

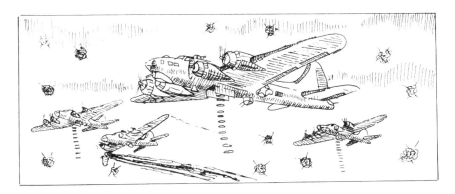

CHAPTER 5: In The Air And On The Sea

Diary From The Front

My husband, Berle M. Robinson, was the radio operator for a B-17 crew stationed in England. They completed 29 combat missions. Excerpts from his letters to his parents created a daily diary.

12-26-44: We are now somewhere in Iceland, but I can't say just where. We had turkey for Christmas dinner, and it was really good. I have some foreign coins, which I'm saving for souvenirs.

1-11-45: I just received my first three letters from United States. I was sure tickled to get them, as I look every day for a letter from home. Makes a guy feel 100 percent better, no fooling. Can't say where I am — but still on my way.

1-30-45: I'm all right, but have begun to wonder if I'm forgotten. I haven't had any mail for more than a week.

2-3-45: Our tour of duty began today. Oxygen was out of operation for the pilot, navigator and engineer. We got flak holes in the bomb bay.

2-6-45: My buddy, Jack Smith, and I went to London to see what it was all about. St. Paul's Cathedral had been hit by a 1,000-pound delayed-action bomb. A Robot Bomb hit the first night we were in town, but it wasn't near us. We ate at the Red Cross Center, as it's good food and as cheap as they can possibly make it. They welcome all the Servicemen and women.

2-20-45: We have flak holes near the tail door and the compass-antenna was severed.

2-23-45: Had a flak-free target today, but made an emergency landing at Woodbridge.

2-25-45: At Munich, Germany, today, the flak was intense. We have two flak holes, one close to my turret.

2-27-45: We got six large flak holes in the wings, and our gasoline line was hit over the target. Never knew how close we came near death: all that was needed was a spark from one of the superchargers, and we would have had it! I really sweated and grew old those hours after bombs-away!

3-9-45: We got a very large hole in the tail section; scared hell out of the tail gunner!

3-11-45: We were the first plane of the 8th Air Force over the target today.

3-17-45: Meager flak, but we had to land in France due to insufficient fuel. Stayed overnight in the town of Merville — flew back to our base the next morning with some news correspondents aboard.

3-24-45: So, they had in the Iowa paper about the Berlin run? Yes, your youngest son was along that day, doing plenty of honest sweating, and thinking how much I'd rather be home. That was the largest raid ever made on Berlin, and some sight! Wish I could say more.

3-25-45: When a plane or crew goes down on a mission and can't communicate, they are considered "missing in action"; 72 hours later their folks are notified. If you ever get this message — disregard it, as most usually a guy gets to neutral land.

3-26-45: Will be looking for your package — the one with the peanuts, 'cause I'm sure hungry for some.

3-27-45: We were up at 0100 in order for our aircraft to drop the bombs in coordination with the BIG drive.

3-30-45: An aircraft exploded as we were forming. We lost the formation . Weather was very bad.

3-31-45: This mission got to me. The sky was black; the target of oil storage and processing was rough. We got 10 flak holes; one crew had over 100 holes. Two aircraft did not return, but they both landed on the Continent.

4-5-45: We went to 29,000 feet to clear the clouds — using so much power that we had to land near Leige, Belgium, at an emergency field to obtain more fuel.

4-11-45: Saw three B-17s hit by flak and explode. We counted several parachutes from one aircraft and four from another. Saw a fighter explode, too. Bandits were all over the area, and one jet plane made a pass at us.

4-12-45: We had a visual target with good results — no flak — no fighters. Had a shower, shave and washed my head — so tonight I feel pretty fresh, with clean clothes. An English lady about half a mile away does my washing every week. It's expensive, but she does a good job, and I'm thankful for that. (It costs at least $2.)

4-19-45: Saw Carlsbad, Czechoslovakia, today. Today was one more mission to our credit. It won't be many days until I'm through over here. If they will allow me to, I'll send a message the day I get my 35 missions done. Excellent bombing results on the visual run today.

4-23-45: I may not get home as soon as I figured, as they are planning to send us to a flak home to rest our nerves.

5-6-45: Flew mercy mission to Holland — dropped food to the civilians near Amsterdam, who were starving at the rate of 1,000 deaths per day. Area is occupied by the Germans, but they agreed to the drop, so there was no shooting by either side. We made the drop between 150- and 100-feet altitude.

Thousands of people were cheering and waving flags as we made our run. We could see the German soldiers shaking their fists at us.

5-8-45: Suppose you've all heard that today was V-E Day, and the combat is finished. Lots of guys were out celebrating way late last night, and it was like the Fourth of July.

5-19-45: Today we flew to Austria to evacuate French prisoners of war. We saw lots of ruined cities that were the results of the 8th Air Force bombings.

Some of the POWs had been behind wire since 1940, and they sure had rough treatment. When we landed in France, lots of people were there to meet them; it was quite a sight! They all wanted to shake hands and salute us.

5-20-45: Right now we have a 14-day training program; we don't know what they have in store for us; we may go to the Pacific Theater of war.

Hope C. Robinson
Yale, Iowa

The Doolittle Raid — A First Person Account

His auto license began with the letters PW because he was a former prisoner of war. This unassuming man, Thomas C. Griffin of Cincinnati, Ohio, took part in the Doolittle Mission of April 18, 1942, which is said to have changed the course of history. Equally important to Americans everywhere, and in every time, it exemplifies the meaning of genuine patriotism and true heroes' mettle.

It was a rare privilege to hear from a participant's lips the detailed and personal account of the Doolittle Raid, sometimes referred to as "Thirty Seconds Over Tokyo." Tom Griffin graduated from the University of Alabama, where he gained his first military training in the Reserve Officers Training Corps, ROTC. After further training, he joined the U.S. Army Air Corps.

A few weeks after the Pearl Harbor attack, Tom's unit, the 17th Bomb Group, was sent to South Carolina. It was there that the Army asked for secret-mission volunteers. Tom said, "Twenty crews from our group were sent to Eglin Field in the Florida Panhandle; there we learned that Jimmy Doolittle would lead us on this mission."

Tom Griffin smiled as he said, "He was known as Jimmy to the public, but we soldiers called him 'sir' and 'colonel.' I still call him general to his face, but here at my kitchen table, I call him Jimmy."

Tom Griffin continued his account of preparations for carrying out the still-secret mission. "Doolittle trained us to take B-25 bombers off an aircraft carrier's deck. This had never been done before. To take a fully loaded B-25 off at 400 feet instead of 1,200 — that was the trick.

"President Roosevelt wanted to retaliate immediately for the

Japanese attack on Pearl Harbor. The only way at that time to get at the Japanese main islands was by long-range Billy Mitchell bombers taking off from a carrier deck. That's what we trained for, and that's what we did."

Tom moved on to California. "On the last day of March, 1942," he remembered, "we flew over to the Naval Air Station in San Francisco Bay. Our planes were loaded on the deck of the *USS Hornet*; the next morning we sailed with our cruisers and destroyers, headed west toward Japan. That was really the only offensive task force the Navy had in the Pacific. If it had been intercepted and sunk, the whole history of World War II would have been different.

"Eighty men volunteered. Sixteen planes were on the deck of the carrier, with five men in each crew. Jimmy Doolittle was with us all the time at Fort Eglin, and he was with us on the *Hornet*. He took the first plane off the carrier. I was a navigator on the ninth plane off the deck. All planes took off quite well.

"Twelve of our 16 bombers had targets in Tokyo, and all but one bombed their targets. One was set upon by so many Japanese planes that they had to jettison their bombs and get out of there."

The plan was to fly to Nationalist China after bombing Japan, and turn the U.S. planes over to Chiang Kai-Shek for use, but it wasn't to be. Tom Griffin explained: "The weather was disintegrating up ahead. Four of our planes ditched along the China coast, and 11 of us pulled up into the storm. Some of those who bailed out had a hard time getting through the Japanese lines; most made it, but eight were captured by the Japanese.

"Our plane had been in the air for 15 and one-half hours; we ran out of gas and had to bail out. None of our crew had ever bailed out before, and we had to parachute out at night in a raging storm."

Tom put it mildly when he said, "That was an unusual experience.

"After a week, our crew finally got together in a village and were taken prisoner by what turned out to be friendly forces of the Chinese army. Survivors of the Doolittle Raid got through to Chungking, headquarters of the Nationalist Chinese."

After his harrowing experiences in Asia, Tom Griffin went on leave, and was reunited with a young lady named Esther. They were married in 1945 and had two sons.

What did Tom Griffin think of things today? He said, "It is my hope that the challenge the Japanese have given us regarding the economy will spur us on to make U.S. products the greatest and best in the world."

Spoken as a true patriot.

Marcia Baker Pogue
Cincinnati, Ohio

NOTE: *A news item from* The Christian Science Monitor *read: "Retired General James Doolittle, whose daring daylight bombing raid on Japan during World War II stunned the Japanese and lifted American morale, died on September 27, 1993. (Age 96 or 97.) General Doolittle was a recipient of the Presidential Medal of Freedom in 1989, the Medal of Honor and many other awards."*

Bogies At Sunset

It was late in 1943 — when the United States began taking the initiative in the Pacific, and the Allies were flexing their muscles — that I received my memorable letter from President Roosevelt.

I was lucky; instead of the usual five days after taking my physical, we were given 10 days before reporting for permanent duty. Christmas was in that 10 days. We were the first contingent with children to be drafted from Fort Worth.

In boot camp, I was fortunate enough to secure a third-class petty officer rating. I did not realize what a boost that was until I saw what other less fortunate men had to do. After a couple of weeks on Ford Island, I was assigned to a carrier aircraft service unit at Kaneobe Bay on the island of Oahu, across from Honolulu.

On returning from liberty at Honolulu one evening in November, I was met at the barracks by my chief, who said: "The lieutenant wants to see you — he has shipping papers for you to report to the carrier *Shangri-La*, I think."

My heart hit the deck with a thud. The condolences of my buddies didn't help much. With considerable misgivings, I reported to the lieutenant. He was very understanding, but explained that the "big push" was on, and it was just a matter of time until the entire unit would be moved. He also told me the ship was not the *Shangri-La*, of which we had heard a great deal, but the *USS Steamer Bay* CVE 87, one of the 50 Kaiser-built escort carriers commonly called a "kaiser kofin." As it turned out, it was the luckiest break I could have had.

At the supply office, we were welcomed with open arms and a sigh of relief. It seems the *Steamer Bay* had been used in ferry service to take surplus planes out to the forward area for other carriers. Now she was to get her own squadron and join the fleet as an operating unit. We were part of the crew necessary to keep the squadron flying. I had recently been made a second-class petty officer, and with this transfer was the highest aviation storekeeper rate on ship. I was given charge of all aviation stores. In addition, we rated a first class, and at the end of four months in rate, I received my first-class rate. This was the lucky break I mentioned previously, which only happens during wartime.

We had some of the finest supply officers possible. I still write to my immediate superior officer. Edwards, the ship's original crew aviation storekeeper third class, was a young boy from South Carolina. He had only book learning about his job, but he knew his way around the ship. What an asset that was. Within minutes he had us secured in the aviation storeroom with cots and lockers, where it was reasonably cool. And in a matter of hours we were initiated to that great Navy game "Kumshaw": to get things done, you scratch my back, I'll scratch yours.

Before leaving Hawaii, there was much speculation as to where we were going. Having a squadron aboard, we knew we were bound for action. MacArthur had landed at Leyte in the Philippines, and a task force of Jeep carriers similar to ours was almost annihilated by the Japanese Fleet at Leyte Gulf making its last big splurge. The gallant stands of these almost defenseless jeep carriers were largely responsible for the Japanese turning tail and running when they almost had victory in their hands. From sitting ducks, the jeeps became Wasps, shooting their pea shooters and launching squadron after squadron into the attack. The planes expended all their bombs and ammunition then made dry runs over the Jap ships to harass them. Out of gas, and no carrier on which to land, many splashed into the sea to be rescued later by destroyers.

Shortly after leaving Pearl Harbor, and into our cruising zig-zag pattern, the captain announced over the ship's speaker system that we were headed for Manus Island in the Admiralties, about 100 miles north of New Guinea. Manus Island and surrounding areas had been secured, but had been the scene of intense fighting some months back. The struggle for New Guinea was still going on. It seemed we were headed right into the tiger's mouth.

The two weeks it took us to get to Manus were busy ones. We had one G.Q. submarine alarm, which could have been a whale. The destroyers hovered over their contact for several hours after dropping depth charges. If it was a sub, it could not be confirmed, but it gave us our first taste of the possibility of an enemy. We were not just play acting.

By Christmas day, the entire task force had gathered: 12 jeep carriers, six older battleships, such as the *Colorado* and *Texas*, innumerable destroyers, destroyer escorts and other ships necessary to make up Task Force No 7. Every attempt was made to have a jovial Christmas, with Santa Claus, a Christmas tree and all the trimmings, but thoughts of the morrow hung over us. My own thoughts were of my wife and boy and whether I would get to see them again. It was with a heavy heart that we went to bed. Lights out came early that night as we were to leave at dawn the next morning.

On January 1, 1945, we left the Papaus. Shortly after clearing the harbor, the captain announced that we were the bombardment group, three days in advance of a landing to be made on Lygayan Gulf on the northern tip of the island of Luzon, Philippines. This meant that to get there we had go through the Philippine Islands, held on both sides by the Japs. We were going to have some action!

At dawn on January 3rd we sighted the Philippines. We had

considerable consternation in our hearts. Next day, gun watches were put on a four-hour on, four-off basis, with the balance of the ship's crew going about normal operations.

I went to evening chow early, as did most of the rest of the crew. I don't think anyone intended to be late for G.Q. this sunset. I know I felt safer up on the flight deck than down below. I was almost through eating when the loud speakers blared out "All flight-deck personnel report to the flight deck on the double — repeat — all flight-deck personnel report to the flight deck on the double." I hurriedly finished eating then started up the ladder to my gun station when, *Waaooo! Waaooo! Waaooo!* — that blood-chilling G.Q. horn blasted out.

Emerging upon the passageway along the flight deck, I looked out across the sea and stopped, dumfounded. There was the *Ominay Bay*, completely on fire, with smoke and flames jumping hundreds of feet in the air.

A Japanese suicide plane with a Kamikaze pilot had dived right out of the sun into the *Ominay Bay*. The ship was hit without warning, apparently unprepared — its radar had failed to pick up the Jap plane in time. For the Japs it was a perfect hit, right at the conning tower and forward elevator. Their bomb exploded and scattered burning gasoline over the flight deck, down onto the hangar deck, then down to the aviation gasoline tanks. In a matter of minutes, the whole front half of the ship was a blazing inferno.

We stood helpless 1,000 yards away — the *Ominay Bay* was burning in the position where less than two hours before we had been stationed.

As our formation turned to get out of the area, we passed very close to the doomed ship. Men were running everywhere; some were jumping overboard. The flames were getting higher, and ammunition began to explode. Destroyers and destroyer escorts edged up to help, but it was hopeless. Soon the order was given to abandon ship. It is hard to imagine the confusion that must have occurred aboard her. To us, standing there spellbound and helpless, it was a sad sight, frustrating to the point of anger.

More men were jumping overboard and climbing upon life

rafts. The flames shot higher, but still the gallant ship showed no signs of sinking — just a flaming raft of fire, smoke and explosions. We watched long past dark. G.Q. was secured, but we talked only in whispers. I did not have the heart to watch after the order was given to sink the ship with torpedoes. I went to my storeroom and waited as did a great many others. A buddy told me when the torpedo struck, a huge ball of fire rose up into the sky, then darkness as the ship sank below the water, the most awesome thing he had ever seen.

This chronicle cannot be concluded without the highest praise for my ship, the *Steamer Bay*, and all her sister ships. Admiral Gallery, in his book *Eight Bells,* expressed his sentimental feeling for his ship CVE *USS Guadalcanal* and its exploits in the Atlantic. His words, as fine as they are, were just a prologue to the honor that should be given these gallant ships and their crews.

I have often wondered what has happened to these unsung heroes, the CVEs. I hope that somewhere one has been anchored as a monument, so that I may take my grandkids to see her and say, "That is a real hero." Somewhere up in that heaven for ships, I know the old *Steamer Bay* is looking down with a wink in her eye saying, "See, I knew I'd get you back, the bogies will always be 'just over the horizon.'"

Nat H. Neville
Submitted by Rubye Neville
Tulsa, Oklahoma

Kamikaze Attacks

We had been at sea over a month when we dropped anchor off the Okinawan shore in July 1945. Although the island was secured in June, our incoming outfit was to man the huge new air base being built to launch B-29 attacks on the Japanese homeland.

Spread out in all directions were huge numbers of American warships. These ships were vulnerable to deadly kamikaze attacks.

Japanese kamikaze pilots were young boys, who were trained to fly small planes that carried one bomb on a one-way suicide flight. Their objective was to dive their planes into our ships. Whole armadas of kamikazes attacked our fleet. That tactic had been used successfully, and the loss of ships and lives had been horrendous.

We assembled, complete with backpacks, and began to descend the nets into landing craft alongside when mayhem broke out all over. Air-raid alert sirens sounded throughout the fleet. Loudspeakers blared, "All troops back aboard. All troops below decks." Gunfire came from all quarters.

All our ships immediately laid down a heavy smoke screen to hide themselves from incoming aircraft. The sky became a gigantic cauldron of death, as all anti-aircraft guns sent up a continual barrage of fire and tracers, leaving a fiery pattern across the sky. To those of us observing, it was a tremendous fireworks display that we weren't permitted to watch very long.

As far as we knew, no ships were lost, but for the Japanese pilots, their mission had been a one-way trip to death.

That raid was a last-gasp attack. The Japanese were out of fuel, out of planes and out of pilots. We had witnessed the last big kamikaze attack of World War II. Within two months the war was over.

Several months later, I was called out one night to help refuel planes on the line. A big transport landed, and a group of gaunt, sick-looking American servicemen unloaded and were taken to a nearby Quonset hut. We learned that they were some of the first repatriated prisoners of war from Japanese prison camps, heading home at last.

So often, we are witnesses to great historic events without realizing or appreciating what we have seen.

Leonard Kristiansen
as told to Jean Kristiansen
Nashua, Iowa

Thirty Hours in the Deep

M. D. "Spiz" Hoffman tells of his naval experiences.

"During World War II, I was a cook on a destroyer, the *USS Hull*. Our ship and crew had been through many battles with the Japanese, but the most memorable incident was a conflict with our arch-enemy Mother Nature's typhoon.

It was December 18, 1944; our fleet had been quietly sailing in the Pacific when storm clouds began to gather. Weather reports were seldom available to us. After several hours, the old ship began to rock, riding high on the waves. It would tip and become almost horizontal. It became evident that this was not an ordinary storm but a full-fledged typhoon.

The captain ordered the crew inside the ship. We could not reach the doors. Along with others I was thrown against the rails, then back against the ship. A sudden lunge of the old ship threw me — and most of the crew — overboard and far into the sea. I was covered with giant waves. Several times I sank, then came to the surface. I could see debris and shipmates all around me. I fought to keep my head above water. I rode the waves until I was exhausted. Then the winds became calmer, and I began to float. I was surprised that I was still wearing my life jacket.

I was floating when I noticed a comrade in the water nearby. We latched onto each other, and it was comforting to have someone with me. We clung to each other for several hours. I noticed that he became very still. He was dead. Hesitantly, I released him. I felt lonely, and many hours passed with no sign of survivors or ships. I knew that I was going to die.

I considered throwing away my life jacket; I knew that death would come quicker that way. I struggled to overcome the thought and continued riding the waves, but the thought persisted. When dark came, I unfastened my life jacket and threw it into the sea. I expected death to come swiftly, but it did not: I continued to float. After several hours, a mattress floated by. I grabbed for it and climbed on. Much to my surprise, it didn't sink. I gave in to my exhaustion, fell lifeless on the mattress, and I was soon asleep.

I was awakened by the noise of a ship. I looked up and saw the *USS Taberer*. The crew dragged my limp body onto their ship. I am sure that I did not look like a human being. I was discolored from the buffeting on the ship and red from sunburn. My lips were parched, and my eyes were almost swollen closed.

The crew helped me take a shower to wash off the saltwater. Then I was asked if I could eat some potato soup. I felt that I could have eaten anything! Nothing before or since has tasted as good as that cup of hot potato soup.

Following the storm, I learned that three ships had sunk in the typhoon. There had been some 800 naval personnel aboard them; only 18 had survived. It has been difficult to share this experience. I have only been able to speak of it the past few years. I am just thankful to be alive.

Virginia L. Shaver
Anderson, Missouri

Medals Only Reminders Of Lost Friends

When I was 12 years old, my father, John Ray Barrick, passed away. He was a World War II hero. We didn't find out what the complete story was until we received our dad's war records.

He had mentioned a Purple Heart, and throwing his medals overboard because they were reminders of good friends he'd lost. He was in and out of Veterans Administration Hospitals and died of battle fatigue.

My mother, Esther Barrick, is a real hero in her own right. She was in charge of eight children — five boys and three girls. Times were tough and heartaches were many. I feel like we were all survivors of World War II.

According to the *The Daily Ardmoreite*, Ardmore, Oklahoma:

"Barrick joined the Navy in March 1942 as a 19-year-old fresh out of Healdton, and served until June 1945. Thirty of his 39 months of duty were spent at sea. Records show he twice survived attack, and ships he fought on led strikes on Palai, first and second

Visayas, Manila, Nansei Shoto, Formosa, and Luzon.

"Barrick won the Purple Heart, the Good Conduct Medal, the Navy Unit Commendation Ribbon with bronze star, the American Area Campaign Medal, the Asiatic-Pacific Campaign Medal with three stars and the World War II Victory Medal."

Mary Bone
Wilson, Oklahoma

Brothers Meet On Guam

I'd like to let others know that it was a tremendous thrill to us back home that our two brothers met in Guam during World War II. Certainly a number of years have gone by, but I do remember this: John, older by a year, was in the Navy, serving on the *SS George Clymet*, a transport ship. Bud was a chaplain for the *Statue of Liberty*, 77th Division, 306th Infantry.

The two came home to us. Of course, when Mom learned that the War in the Pacific was over, she expected them to come right home. It took a little longer, though, by several months.

Catherine Heaney
Chicago, Illinois

A Chance Encounter

My father, Thomas Williams, served his time in the Navy during World War II. He was a Seabee, and was stationed in the South Pacific most of the time. I heard many war stories, but this one stuck with me.

My father heard about a beautiful waterfall while he was stationed in Australia. He wanted to see this, so he asked the other guys to go with him. They wouldn't go along. Since he was more or less a loner, he went by himself.

To get to this waterfall he had to go up a very steep hill. It was so steep, he had to get down on his hands and knees to work himself to the top.

Now he could see over the crest of the hill. There stood an Australian native: paint, feathers and all. Daddy couldn't stay where he was, so he moved to where he could stand. Now he was thinking "aborigines." He was never so scared in his life. He just stood and looked at the native. All kinds of things were going through his mind.

The native looked at him, and with his Limey accent said, "Good day, sir."

Dorothy Williams
Hamburg, Pennsylvania

View Of Iwo Jima

In 1943, my draft number came up and I was called to be inducted into the service. I was selected to go into the Navy. I was drafted for overseas service on a troop ship heading for New Caledonia.

After arriving there, I was assigned to a battle damage repair ship, the *USS Oceanious*. Our duty was to repair the damaged ships that would pull along side of us.

We were on several of the islands below the equator. Our ship was assigned duty with the Third Fleet to invade Iwo Jima. We followed the Marines into Iwo Jima. We were within 600 yards of the beach. We could easily see the battle going on between the American armed forces and the Japanese.

After several days of fierce fighting, we witnessed the raising of the American flag over Mount Suribachi, of which there is a statue erected across the Potomac River from Washington, D.C. After 18 days at Iwo Jima we were sent to join the invasion of Okinawa; 72 days later we were sent to join a fleet getting ready for the invasion of Japan.

Saved by the atomic bomb, we did not invade Japan. We ended up in the Philippines when the War ended.

Wilton Swinford
Keokuk, Iowa

"Daylight In The Dark Of Night"

I was a merchant seaman during World War II. I was in a 150-ship convoy from New York City port to Murmansk, Russia. We carried Tiger tanks and large storage batteries for electrical plants. Some were real whoppers.

On the high seas, near the coast of Norway, the convoy was attacked by German U-boats. I was on deck and saw a T-2 tanker and smaller tankers explode. It was like daylight in the dark of night.

August Miller
Downs, Kansas

The Last Voyage Of The Pan Mass

This is the story of a German submarine torpedoing the tanker *Pan Massachusetts* 18 miles from shore at St. Augustine, Florida, on February 19, 1942. A Jacksonville newspaper described it as "the most dramatic ship-sinking of the War."

The ship, commonly known at "The Pan Mass" to mariners of the Gulf of Mexico and Atlantic coasts, was blown apart by two torpedoes, while loaded with over 100,000 barrels of gasoline, kerosene and diesel fuel. It went down in a lake of fire.

Twenty of the crew of 38 perished in the inferno aboard ship or attempting to escape the flaming cargo that spread out over the water. Eighteen others, including the writer, miraculously escaped by diving or jumping off the ship — some without life preservers — making their way past the fire on the water, then swimming in a cold, rough, wind-and rain-swept sea until rescued.

December 3, 1941, to late February 1942 were the first few perilous weeks of World War II, when our merchant ships were obliged to travel our coastal routes unarmed and unescorted. Enemy U-boats lie in wait much of the way; it was a time that came to be described as "the Atlantic coast massacre" and Suicide Alley.

The ship was the first to be sunk by enemy action so near shore during daylight hours; the first to be attacked south of Cape

Hatteras, North Carolina — marking the extension of the U-boat menace southward — and the 31st of more than 270 cargo ships that would be sunk in our Atlantic coastal waters before the War's end.

Torpedoes from the German U-boat transformed the ship into a roaring inferno, the surrounding sea into a lake of fire. Six of us were trapped far below in the engine room by flame and smoke. Three perished; three escaped.

We made it to the fantail, encircled by a flaming sea littered with dead and dying men. It was every man for himself. The ship was believed to be going down. By a lucky turn of fate, it became possible to dive off and make it past the flames on the water. Then came the hours of struggle in the cold, rough sea without a life preserver. Finally, rescue came at sundown. We were rescued by the crew of a British freighter and put ashore at Jacksonville, Florida, the following day. Ten of us were hospitalized.

As I checked out of the hospital one week after admittance, the only one of us remaining there, George Fox, was on the critical list and under heavy sedation. Two days later came a happy reunion with my beloved wife and daughter. One day in 1947, I again encountered George Fox, in a surprise meeting on a ship in the Houston Turn Basin.

> By Joe L. Wright
> submitted by Inez Wright
> Louisville, Kentucky

Typhoon At Okinawa

A lasting memory will be the typhoon at Okinawa in October 1945. I was engineering officer aboard the *USS YMD 291*, a wooden-hulled minesweeper, anchored in Buckner Bay.

As predicted, the storm steadily increased. I was officer of the deck and in charge of the watch; at 1600 hours I checked the anchor and assessed the wind velocity.

By observing the surrounding vessels, it was apparent that the force of the wind was affecting a major supply ship that was anchored near our *YMS*. The supply vessel was dragging anchor, and we were quickly being forced into a precarious position in relation to the much larger supply ship.

I immediately alerted our captain, proceeded to order anchor aweigh and put our ship underway to prevent a mishap. Now we had to ride out the storm by evading and preventing collision with other ships, some firmly anchored, some fighting it out.

Visibility was nearly zero for the next 12 hours; wind velocity peaked at 153 miles per hour; heavy seas crashed thunderously, and salt spray went over the flying bridge where we stood in control of our small minesweeper.

During the siege of the storm, our skillful captain was on the conn, and everyone was on watch for fear of collision, aground or capsize. The typhoon roared and raged at ships and men.

As the long night wearied on, the storm somewhat abating, I knew that our skipper would soon reach the point of physical exhaustion, and one of us should be alert and prepared to conn the ship. Even though the decks were sloshy — and equipment was crashing about freely as lashings were torn away — I used my life jacket for a pillow and propped myself in a corner of the pilot house. I was soon warm and dry and actually went to sleep.

At dawn I was awakened by a refreshed shipmate who was ready to take charge of the ship safely and protect the lives of the other officers and crew. All around were some 150 ships, capsized or aground. Some ships had sunk, with loss of life. We had experienced hearing their frantic messages, their last commands and words of farewell via our ship-to-ship frequency as they prepared to abandon ship. Through the next day we were delegated to cruise the area, survey the loss of shipping and appraise the damage that was suffered by our Mine Pac Division at Buckner Bay, Island of Okinawa.

From our fleet of some 20 like vessels, we were one of the three surviving with no loss, damage, or injury.

Galen C. Robinson
Marion, Iowa

150

CHAPTER 6: Women At War

Moz, A Pioneer Woman Pilot

Mozelle Simpson was a member of the Women Armed Service Pilots in 1943. She trained the male bombardiers who were in turn sent overseas for the fighting effort. Information regarding her was still classified as late as 1982, but we can now tell how she flew four-engine bombers.

The following excerpts are from an article that ran in our town newspaper three months before Mozelle I. Simpson died.

"Mozelle flew more than 2,000 hours in twin-engine planes and earned her wings not only from the WASPs, but also from the United States Army Air Force.

"Letters to her sister, Lillian Pipkin, also of Quitman, tell of her many flying hours. They also tell of the varied reactions of the men who would stand out by the airplanes talking to her while waiting for the 'pilot' to show up.

"Her happiest hours were spent in 'my honey' as she called it, and whenever she had the opportunity to fly near family, she would 'buzz' their house. 'We even had signals worked out,' said Lillian."

In a time when a woman's place was considered to be in the home, and bombardiers expected their training instructor pilots to be men, Mozelle carved out a place for herself in the history of women's aviation.

Mrs. Geneva Fairbanks
Rossville, Kansas

Getting By

My family lived in Arkansas when World War II was declared. I remember very well how much our family was upset when my dad got his call to serve his country.

Our grandparents, aunts and uncles lived 70 miles away. My parents decided that Mama and her kids — all six of us — should move closer to our relatives. Mama knew it would be a struggle for all of us without Daddy.

It took most of the day traveling to reach our new home, which was an old farmhouse out in the country. The farmer who owned the old house was a very kind man. He had a large field of corn and black-eyed peas. He let my brother and me pick peas on the half. We also picked pumpkins and popcorn. We had quite a supply put away for the winter.

We went to a one-room country school. It was cold walking to school, even though Mama made me wear those long cotton socks, which I hated. After I got out of sight of my mom, I would roll them down around my ankles, trying to make them look like the pretty anklets that some of the girls were wearing. One day on the way home from school we were caught in a rain storm. I was wearing a purple crepe dress. The wetter I got, the more my dress shrank. It kept shrinking and shrinking, until it was far above my knees. I was very embarrassed.

During the war there was a shortage of rubber. We couldn't buy elastic, even if we had the money. We cut strips of tire inner tubes for garters to hold our stockings up. We also used these strips of rubber for the elastic in our bloomers, which were made from feed sacks and white flour sacks. The printed flour sacks Mama saved, until she had enough of the same print to make a dress for one of us girls. We made our own hair curlers by cutting strips of tin from a Pet milk can. We wrapped these strips of tin with paper and we had curlers for our hair.

There was a stock pond behind my aunt's house. We had fun going down there and finding duck eggs. One warm spring day, we decided to take my aunt's washtubs and use them for boats. A tub turned over with my little sister in it. When we got her out from under the tub, she was gasping for breath. We got the scare of our lives.

Mama's health began to fail. She was sick a lot. With the help of the Red Cross, Mama's doctor got Daddy out of the service. My brother took the old truck to the bus station to pick up my dad. My little sister remembers wondering who that handsome man in uniform was with our brother when they drove up in front of our house. It was a happy homecoming. Daddy went to work as a machinist in an airplane plant. Mama regained her health. One year later we had a new little sister, and after her we had a new little brother.

Chris Zejda
Perryton, Texas

Life As A Lady Marine

I was in the Marine Corps, Camp Lejeune, North Carolina, from August 1943 to November 1945. My parents had also said goodbye to my brother in June. He served during World War II in the Army under Patton.

One of my reasons for leaving, in addition to patriotism, was to get away from a problem boyfriend. After serving two years in North Carolina, and being around so many Marines, he looked pretty good to me. I came home and married him, and we had 34 years together before his death in 1980.

Here are some highlights of being a lady Marine:

With 6,000 men on base and only 2,000 women, we did not lack for dates, but many of the men thought we were there for their pleasure, so on each date that battle had to be fought. In each case, I was given the respect that I asked for, but it was quite an education in life.

Living in a barracks with 60 other women was also an education. I learned about different races, religions and lifestyles. My job was in the same building where I lived, so I only had to go down the hall to my typing job in the Women Marines Company Office. I worked my way through clerk typist, muster roll clerk, payroll clerk and finally into acting first sergeant, with my own company of 100 women. It was very good for my self esteem to learn that I could do things that I never believed I could.

Holidays on the base were especially deadly, but we were all in the same boat, so we planned things to do. When I would go home, I was astonished at the lovely colors in my home after being used to olive drab. I declared I'd never wear a hat again, because dress code required we wear one everywhere.

It was a huge base with six movie theaters — all free, so we saw lots of good movies. I met some skaters, who taught me a lot about skating, which I loved. That also was free on the base.

On weekends off the base or on a three-day pass, a group of us would visit the various towns around Camp Lejeune. I would try to learn all I could about each town and the various churches and denominations there.

We could go to the mess hall and request a picnic lunch in our off-duty hours, so often we would get bikes (also free) and ride to the beach or woods for a picnic. Swimming in the ocean was quite an interesting thing for this country gal, who knew nothing about salt water, beaches or sun bathing.

Sometimes the Coast Guard would arrange a party with food for us, and take us deep-sea fishing. Farther inland was an island where we could go canoeing. On the base were recreation halls for ping pong, card playing and various games to pass the time.

We could also meet in the laundry room, where each girl was required to wash, dry and iron her own summer uniform. Winter drab or olive-green uniforms went to the cleaners free. Cuban-heel shoes were regular wear, until later, when we were issued medium-heel pumps. The shoe cobbler on base took care of those repairs, but we learned to spit and polish them along with the best Marines.

We each had our regular cleaning duty the night before inspection, as well as on a daily basis. Demerits were issued if anyone did not meet the strict standards.

We each signed up for the duration and up to six additional

months. We received our honorable discharge according to a point system that considered rank, length of duty and such. We were allowed to sign up for duty in Hawaii, the only overseas duty open to us during World War II. I thought life was hard enough here and had no desire to go anywhere else. We were issued mustering-out pay and a ruptured duck; a dove symbol to wear, telling the world we were discharged. I was one happy person going home, but it was a very interesting and educational 27 months.

Joan Baker Falke
Des Moines, Iowa

Mother Of Five Kansas Sailors Christens Navy Ship

This article is an excerpt from *The Kansas City Star*, July 24, 1942:

"With firm swing, Mrs. Rena Fairbanks of Emmett, Kansas, shatters a bottle of champagne against the *USS Chickasaw*, Navy fleet tug at a San Francisco shipyard. Frank Fairbanks, her husband, is in the left foreground intent upon his wife's efficient performance of the task. The Navy honored Mrs. Fairbanks by inviting her to San Francisco to sponsor the auxiliary ship because five of her sons wear its uniform. One of them, Carl, was aboard a ship sunk in the Java Sea and is reported missing. The launching ceremony was held last night."

Geneva Fairbanks
Rossville, Kansas

Doing One's Patriotic Duty

I was in my senior year of college in 1943 at Springfield, Missouri. We were at war, and many of my male contemporaries had joined some branch of the military, so school was not as interesting as in prior years. I had been cramming for term finals and felt that I needed a break, so I opted for a movie, *On the Shores of Tripoli*. It was a story about a selfish fellow who joined the Marines as a lark, and the Marines made a man out of him. I enjoyed the movie, and it made one think of patriotic duty — especially since we were at war.

At the end of the movie there was a newsreel showing one of the first graduating classes of Navy women — all nattily attired in navy blue and marching sharply along. This was followed by a huge screen-sized picture of Uncle Sam pointing straight at me with the words, "I need you." I made up my mind right then and there that I would join the Marines, thus releasing a man to fight at sea. I jumped on a bus to get to the post office and locate the recruiting office. I announced that I wanted to join the Marines.

A very patient recruiter explained that the Navy trained the Marines, but upon completion of training, one had the option of joining the Marine Corps. That was OK by me, so I filled out the papers he produced and left with some forms for a doctor to fill out after giving me a physical. Two days later I returned these papers and was told that they would start processing my application. A few weeks later I received orders to take a train to St. Louis for pre-processing. I was amazed to find three train cars crammed with jabbering women, all going to St. Louis for the same reason.

A bus met the train, and we were whisked to a big federal building. We were ushered into a large room where we were given a battery of tests — reading, math, English, geography, history and a smattering of physics. We got back home late that evening tired, but with high, expectant hopes.

I continued with school but kept in touch with some of my new friends. Before long, one by one received orders to a Navy training school, but none came for me. I began to worry, so I journeyed to the recruiting office, but they told me to stop fretting, my orders would get to me eventually. Time marched on and still no orders. I kept pestering that poor recruiter, until he finally agreed to investigate the status of my application.

After a few days the recruiter called to tell me that I had been selected for officer training, and orders would be issued after I had graduated and furnished the Navy with my graduate credentials.

When I finally received my orders to Mount Holyoke College in Massachusetts, I left two days early. I had heard that war-time travel was unpredictable, and I didn't want to run the risk of being AWOL. I arrived early, and no one knew what to do with an early arrival, but I was finally given a room.

When the rest of the girls arrived, we got acquainted fast since we knew we were going to spend a lot of time together. They all thought I was a real Missouri square when they learned that I had joined the service for purely patriotic reasons. Others, we learned, joined to get away from home, to change jobs, to do something different or to find a husband. Despite their snickering I stood by my patriotic feelings, and I still stand by them. I cannot listen to our national anthem without getting all choked up, goose pimples on my arms and neck and a queer knot in my middle near my heart.

Some think I'm a sentimental fool, but it makes me feel good to think it's just that old black magic of patriotism.

Cmdr. Evelyn N. (Dene) Sooy
U.S. Naval Reserve (Retired)
San Diego, California

Security Tight At Ordnance Plants

When the Japanese bombed Pearl Harbor on December 7, 1941, the United States entered the War immediately. During those years it was hard to realize the immensity of the War — but the fear, trauma and sadness were always there. There was no television, so we got our news from papers, the radio, newsreels before a picture show and word of mouth from the families who had heard from a loved one. As I think back, it was like being on an emotional roller coaster.

I had just graduated from high school in the spring of 1941. As more and more young men were called into the service, jobs became more plentiful. I held various jobs before a girl friend and I went to visit my oldest brother in western Iowa. The Nebraska Ordnance Plant at Mead was hiring, so we went to work out there. We stayed in a dormitory, where there was a big cafeteria, recreation hall, post office, etc. It was like a small town.

We rode a bus to the line we worked on. In a locker room we had to take off our clothes, then line up naked to be searched by a guard matron. Next, we dressed in their clothes, which included a coverall uniform. Since we were working on bombs, no matches or metal of any kind — not even bobby pins in our hair — was allowed on the line. Nothing that might cause a spark that would set off the powder was allowed. I worked mostly at the beginning of the line where the bombs were painted, and did lots of moving with fork-lift trucks. As you got closer to the area where the powder was, the trucks were electric.

This was a learning experience, but it was also a fun time for me. Twice weekly a bus took us from our dormitory to the small town of Wahoo, which was nearby. The bus also took us to Omaha on the weekends for shopping, and we saw some stage shows featuring well-known stars and musical groups. This was a treat for a small town girl!

I will always remember Christmas 1943. It was the first time my friend and I had ever been away from home at Christmas, and we were both homesick. On Christmas morning, a father came to pick up his two daughters. He said, "Come on home with us," and needless to say, we went. They welcomed us with love and a big traditional meal, and we sure appreciated it.

Eventually, it was necessary for me to move back home with my mother in Illinois. I got a job at the Iowa Ordnance Plant in Burlington. All the workers there were bused in from all the little towns for miles around. We got on the bus at 10 p.m., worked from midnight until 8 a.m., then went back home at 10 a.m. the next morning. We went through the same procedure as we did in Nebraska before we went to our job on the detonator line. The line consisted of small rooms called bays, with one machine in each bay. Each machine was a wheel — completely enclosed — with four small openings. Each opening was covered with heavy glass, with just enough room to put your arms inside to work. One girl put the detonator on the wheel, and two more girls put a tiny scoop of powder in it as it went by. The powder was leveled off with a rubber band stretched across the cup. The fourth girl packed them, and another girl carried little cups of powder to the line. One girl dropped a cup of powder one night. It exploded, but it was not in our bay. The potential danger kept everyone awake and careful.

On August 14, 1945, we heard the news that the Japanese had surrendered. We went to work that night, but nobody did any work — we just celebrated. We were laid off immediately.

My husband-to-be served in the Army in Maui, Molakai, the Philippines, New Guinea and Japan. He was a mortar crewman and a radio and switchboard operator; he drove jeeps and Army trucks and was in Special Services.

B. Alice Holtsclaw
Hamilton, Illinois

Through The Eyes Of A Child

I was 2 years old when Britain entered World War II on Sunday, September 3, 1939. Growing up in Kent, in southeast England, normal life for me was nightly air raids with streets and houses bombed and burning. Food was scarce; I was so thin that my shoulder blades stuck out. I called them my angel wings.

Four months after the start of war in Britain, food was rationed. The weekly ration allowed each person one ounce of cheese, two ounces of margarine, four ounces of bacon, one egg and 10-pence worth of meat. My mother sometimes used her egg to bake a cake. Mum tried to explain that there had not always been war and that it would end some day. I was too young to understand a way of life of which I had no recollection, so I thought she was wrong. I believed that people had to be killed in war or they would get too old. War was how people died.

I wondered why she didn't understand. I was never scared; I thought I had to take care of adults, who feared the raids. When the warning sirens wailed, my grandmother was always terrified.

"Oh dear, oh dear, what shall we do?" she kept repeating as she ran in circles.

I would catch her and reach up for her hand to lead her outside to the shelter. We each had to take our ration book, identity card, gas mask and a blanket.

All windows were made light-proof with sheets of black paper. Once outside, we stumbled down the garden path in darkness.

One night my parents lingered outside in the moonlight to observe an unusually low-flying aircraft, seemingly without markings. As they wondered which side it was on, the pilot opened fire on them. Dad pushed Mum through the shelter entrance and dived in after her.

The Anderson Shelters issued to 6 million families were built into the ground and covered with earth. The only entrance was a narrow door. A crate inside served as a step down to the earth floor. Bunk beds lined the walls. When the door was closed, we were in complete darkness unless my parents lit a candle. The light flickering on the arched corrugated steel soon revealed glistening condensation trickling down the metal furrows. A musty odor was always present in the dampness. Sometimes my parents opened the door to watch planes in fight and flight. The little doorway was like a television screen showing a sky lit by searchlights and explosions. My parents' bodies were dark silhouettes against the glowing sky.

My father often rode his bicycle to the next town to check on family members after a raid. One night, when the sky in their direction was alight with the blaze of burning buildings, he didn't wait until the end of the raid. He found the entire street behind my uncle's home burning.

Dad worked the day shift in the munitions factory. Bombs often hit the factory, which was built on marshland. Luckily, the bombs passed through the floor to the bog below. The men roped off each hole in the floor and continued working. Dad enlisted in the Local Defense Volunteers, soon renamed the Home Guard, and was issued an Enfield rifle. Often, in the worst of the night bombings, he didn't remember walking home. I thought he sometimes made it home while in his sleep.

Several bombs fell close to our home, leaving craters and

exposing chalk under the topsoil. One bomb fell a few yards from our house without detonating. Dad disassembled it in his garden workshop. My mother watched from the kitchen window a few feet away, while I begged to look.

Everyone did their part in the war effort. Volunteers filled sandbags used to protect essential services and prevent injury from flying glass. Housewives knitted socks for soldiers, made bandages from ripped sheets and donated anything metal from their homes to be turned into Spitfires. Little boys gave up their lead soldiers, lead roofs were ripped off churches and iron railings were removed from churchyards to be scrapped for munitions. Children collected paper for recycling.

During the early part of the War, 1.5 million children were evacuated to safety. By 1940, more than half had returned home. My family opted to stay together. I carried a gas mask to school every day. Lessons were often disrupted when we had to seek shelter from air raids. Schools and hospitals were often targets. The hospital was bombed as my mother was giving birth to my brother.

World War II shook women out of their formerly dependent, subordinate roles. As fathers, husbands and sons were called up, they left a gap in the male-dominated work force that women had to fill. Thousands of women joined the forces. Others were active in civil defense. They were air-raid wardens, ambulance and fire-truck drivers, shipyard and railway workers. Some became welders, plumbers or electricians.

Mothers left at home felt the most anguish, protecting their children while worrying and waiting for their men. They suffered through endless nights in shelters, only to arise early the next morning to stand in line to purchase food wherever it was available. I remember standing for hours in long food lines with my mother. Often the food ran out before we reached the head of the line, or we lost our place in line taking cover during an air raid.

People stayed home, only going out for food. Entertainment was the "wireless." The radio's first hit song about the War was, "We're Gonna Hang Out the Washing on the Siegfried Line," followed by "Run, Adolph, Run." Any song by Vera Lynn was well-received. A popular children's series ended with the words, "Good night, children, wherever you are," for the children who had been separated from their families.

On June 6, 1944, I saw the sky filled with Allied planes heading out to sea. The drone of aircraft could be heard for hours. This was D-Day. We all hoped that this meant the War would soon be won.

On May 7, 1945, Britain joyously celebrated victory. People sang and danced around bonfires in the streets.

Brenda East
Victor, Montana

Milkweed Pods For The War Effort

In 1944 I was teaching in a small rural school near Cornett, Wisconsin. There were eight grades in Fairview School. That fall the War Department sent out a desperate call for milkweed pods. The fluff of milkweed seed "umbrellas" could be used in Mae West-type life jackets in place of kapok, which was in short supply.

I borrowed a large truck with a stake rack from the Bloomer Bottling Works of Bloomer, Wisconsin. All 44 students climbed onto the truck, and I drove it up to a landmark hill called Baldy Mountain. Milkweed grew on the hill, in nearby fields and along the roads in profusion.

The students poured off the truck, grabbed large mesh bags provided by the War Department and picked thousands of milkweed pods. There was more than one excursion to the area; after each, the brightly colored bags full of pods hung to dry from fence lines on our farm. Fairview School's impressive collection greatly exceeded those of other schools in the area.

A huge van was sent from the county seat, Chippewa Falls, to collect the bags of milkweed pods. They were taken to a processing plant and used in the war effort. One can only wonder. Did this school effort help a serviceman — perhaps in the South Pacific.

Clara Planing Reeve
Cornell, Wisconsin

Loose Garters Sink Hose

I had worked my way through college and had little money to spend on new clothes. Upon graduation in 1943, I received orders for Navy active duty training at Mount Holyoke College in Massachusetts. The Navy worked hard to turn us landlubbers into immediate midshipmen, emerging after 90 days as all-knowing ensigns. Not only did we spend a lot of time in classes, we also held daily drills, marching to the "hup, two" of the drill instructor. One couldn't help but be proud to be one of a ship-shape group of navy blue uniforms, marching en masse, with white-gloved hands swinging back and forth against the navy blue background.

Occasionally the companies of the battalion would parade in precision down the drill field and past a reviewing stand, where our skipper, Capt. Underwood, would stand and return the salutes of our company commander as we strutted by with "eyes right." On one occasion like this we were marching down the field for the review. Since I was a shorty I always ended up in the last row of the company. We executed our final turn and were ready to march past the reviewing stand when I felt a strange sensation in my lower back. Of course, I kept right on marching and swinging my white-gloved hands like everyone else. But all too soon I became aware of *big* trouble — my hose began to sag, and little by little my stockings were slithering down my legs. I realized that the strange feeling was the deterioration of my old garter-belt hooks, which held up my stockings. Soon that tacky garter belt would be dangling between my legs, and eventually I would be tripping on it. I was in a panic. Luckily, there was a large tree right beside our marching path, so I hitched up my skirt front and aft — in a far-from-military posture — and marched right behind that wonderful tree and out of sight of the reviewing stand. I remained hidden there until the parade was over and everyone had left.

I returned to our quarters and secured the offensive garment with a big safety pin. Of course I was told to report to our commanding officer. I explained my strange behavior, expecting full well to be tossed out of the Navy. I'm almost certain that he had a hard time keeping a straight face, but somehow managed a stern countenance. I was sentenced to two weeks on "The Tree" (no liberty) with an admonishment to keep my undergarments in more wearable condition. That was a close one.

Cmdr. Evelyn N. (Dene) Sooy
U.S. Naval Reserve (Retired)
San Diego, California

At The Mines

The open-pit copper mine owned by Phelps Dodge Corporation, at Morenci, Arizona, was a defense plant during World War II. Trucks hauled the rich ore from the pit to the plant. Rock and other debris was separated from the copper-bearing ore, which then was melted in the smelter and poured out as large, flat slabs of copper mixed with small parts of gold and silver. These slabs were shipped on flatbed railroad cars to refineries owned by Phelps Dodge at another location.

My employment at the mine began in February 1943, when a request from the mine came to my high school in Duncan, Arizona, asking for a girl who could work in their construction office. I was called to the principal's office and offered the job. Assured that my grades were good and that I could graduate if I left school to work at the defense plant, I accepted.

The building where I worked had several departments. I saw women from them in the central rest room, but I was the only female clerk in my department. Many men were in the outer room. Some stayed at their drafting boards all day drawing blueprints, while others left to do surveys or outside jobs. My job was in the construction superintendent's office, where I typed, filed papers and answered the telephone.

When construction was finished, I took another job as a clerk in the power plant. It was there that I remember women doing men's work while the men were at war.

During that time, I walked through a picket line one morning

164

to go to my job, and a loud-voiced woman tried to stop me. I pushed her hand off my arm and told her, "I hired out to do a job, and I'm going in to do it." I went on up the steps from the parking lot without any more opposition. I was the only clerk in the power plant that day.

Once someone spotted something high in the sky that seemed to hover in one place. We took turns going to the roof to watch it for several minutes at a time. Was it an enemy spy object? It was too high to tell what it was. Later, we learned that it was a planet closer to Earth than usual.

Then came a day never to be forgotten. The atomic bomb was dropped in Japan! We couldn't listen to the radio at the power plant because of the interference, but when reports were phoned to us, we passed the word to everyone else. Of course, there were no televisions yet, but from the descriptions, it sounded as if the very atmosphere was igniting as predicted in the Bible.

Although that was not the case, it was very sobering; we need to be aware of the horror that even today is locked in those stockpiled atomic bombs.

Soon the War was over, defense plants were not needed; I married my boss, leaving all of that era to memory.

Vivian Skipper
Jamestown, California

Pioneer In Women's Army Corps

I could hardly believe it! A few hours before, I was anticipating adventure, romance and patriotism — on my way by train to the Women's Auxiliary Army Corps. It was January 2, 1943; my destination was Fort Des Moines.

I was sitting on an upper GI bunk listening to a woman officer giving us an Army orientation. We were to call the women officers "ma'am," the male officers "sir." We were required to stay in the Army for the duration plus, unless we had an incurable illness, immoral or undisciplined behavior, or we got ourselves pregnant.

A "yellow" or disgraceful discharge, would be given for all charges except the incurable illness. The officer also mentioned a WAAC guardhouse.

We were to leave the "stables" only on command. We were housed in a former horse stable used by cavalry soldiers who had fought in other wars.

I found myself becoming terrified. How could I memorize all these things about the Army? Instead of feeling the former joy, I felt I was in prison; that "duration plus" sounded like being incarcerated for life!

About 2 a.m., one woman sat up in bed. "To hell with a yellow discharge — I'll get pregnant!" she said.

I was shocked! What had we gotten ourselves into?

After mess the next morning, while we were all meandering around the stables with our mismatched uniforms — still in a bewildered state of mind — the sergeant yelled, "Fall out on the double!" We were hustled outdoors and put through our first paces of drilling. After three hours of drilling, we were dismissed back to the stables. Before we could sit on our bunks and rest after the strenuous exercise, the sergeant snapped, "Gather up everything you own, put it in these duffel bags — we're moving to Boom Town, a mile down the road."

Boom Town was a number of hastily built structures, complete with lower and upper bunks, wall lockers, and foot lockers shaped like trunks.

After we had worked for two hours putting things away neatly, the sergeant threw us some bars of soap. She looked our area over with disgust. "This is Friday. Tomorrow morning, we have inspection. Clean and rinse the floors around your area. If you have anything civilian, give it to me. Your blouses (jackets) are buttoned all the way down. The shirts are also buttoned the same way on hangers. In your foot locker only, GI articles are neatly arranged."

During inspection, the captain gave every bunk a lick with his whip. About three bunks down, he cut the air with a sharp, "Dust on blanket. One gig."

Our steady stares were broken when the commandant put on white gloves, climbed a ladder and found dust on the rafters.

"Everyone a gig," he said, as the sergeant was writing down gigs. When anyone received three gigs, she was confined to the barracks on weekends.

The strain was too much for one WAAC. She fainted. Col. McCoskrie picked her up, his brown eyes pleading to the woman officer, "What should I do?" He gently laid her on her bunk. The officer quickly commanded the sergeant to bring in a wet washrag.

The six weeks of basic training went quickly. The only way we endured it was the expectation of a transfer to an all-male camp. There were only three schools of training here at Fort Des Moines: the MPs, where only WAACs could use judo; Motor Transport, where mechanics were taught; and Cooks and Bakers. We all dreaded the latter as a permanent assignment.

When basic was terminated, we looked for whose names were posted and who was stuck there at the fort.

A few WAACs were sent to men's camps, but most of us were assigned to the fort. Domestic, bed-making Eleanor was an artist, assigned to help an artist-officer paint a mural on the Service Club wall.

My assignment was irrelevant to helping the war effort. I was assigned every morning to cleaning men's and women's latrines, cleaning the Service Club, and on Wednesday, scrubbing, waxing and polishing the ballroom floor.

What broke the dismal fruitlessness of our slave-labor jobs was Warner Brothers filming *Women At War* at the fort. Doris Day and Fay Emerson were the leading ladies; Robert Warwick, the general. Doris Day never wore makeup, except when being filmed, and never caroused with others in the cast at nightclubs.

Fay Emerson had the MPs on the jump. The fort was large, and many didn't know a movie was being filmed. One night an MP stopped Fay, who was out walking around in her Army costume, hair below her collar, a veil over hat, lipstick, chewing gum. The MP was ready to arrest her when an officer interfered and informed the MP about the movie.

We were visited after the Warner Brothers movie by movie star Robert Young. He visited our mess hall, and the women acted as hysterical and wild as they do now over rock singers. The press acted crazy, too. They hung on chandeliers to get pictures of him eating with WAACs. The WAACs thronged around him as he left the mess hall. They ignored the officers' warnings about having his autograph inked on their cuffs and collars.

I think of the women who have come so far — flying in combat and reaching the rank of general. I'm proud and grateful that I pioneered for them as I did.

Alice Amyx Hugo
Tulsa, Oklahoma

A Mother And A Mailman

During World War II while my brother was fighting in North Africa and Italy, my mother made sure she got a letter in the mailbox every day for him. Our home was on a side road, one-quarter of a mile from one crossroad and three-quarters of a mile from the other. Although a mailman went by each corner, because of the location of the post office our mailbox had to be at the three-quarter mile corner, the farthest away. If my mother knew she would be late for the mailman at our box, she would walk to the other corner. Day after day she would walk — sometimes run — to get the letters mailed.

Finally, the mailman at the one-quarter mile corner told her that although it wasn't legal, if she would put a box at the corner and always raise the flag, he would stop and get her letters. That would save her a lot of steps and time. My mother and the mailman have been gone many years, but I often think of the many letters she put in that box, and the many steps that were saved by a kind and thoughtful mailman.

Vera Wells
St. Joseph, Missouri

Devastation In Britain

When World War II broke out in England in 1939, I was living in the suburbs of London in Worcester Park, Surrey, with my mother, father and younger sister. I was just in my early teens, so it seemed so scary to hear the word "war." We had to go to our local school building to pick up our gas masks and be shown how to use them, which was a very scary experience in itself. Everywhere we traveled we had to have our gas masks with us. Many of the children were taken by ships to Australia where they would be safe. By the time my parents decided to let my sister and me go it was too late; the last ship was ready to leave.

In early 1940 we moved from the London area to Penketh, Lancashire. For two years at the beginning of the war we were bombed about every night. My dad would turn a sofa over against a buffet and we would sleep underneath there, away from any flying shrapnel and glass. I can remember the house and dishes shaking from the big ack-ack guns 100 feet from our house. The German planes would follow the Mersey River looking for the big air force base, but although bombs dropped all the way around it, none actually hit the base.

I began working at the air force base for Air Ministry, a government job, at the beginning of 1941. I was secretary to the overseer of the European Theater of War. The office was classified highly secret. Even my father, who worked at the base, had to be escorted to my office by a security guard. In June 1942 all British air force personnel and civilians were shipped out to Europe, and the American Army Air Corps came in and took over the base. Out of 225 English gals, only 12 of us were kept on to work for the Americans. I was lucky to be one of them and became secretary in Col. Ott's office. At the most critical time in the War we were working 24-hour days: all day, all night and all the next day. My husband-to-be and I were stationed at the same base. On July 7, I met him and we started dating. We were married 15 months later on October 25, 1943. Our oldest son was born in Lancashire, England, on July 9, 1945.

At the beginning of 1944 the Germans were sending over robot planes — you would hear the drone of the engines and then nothing, you would just sit waiting for the boom when the plane dropped. One dropped two houses from us once.

Another time we were on a bus coming home from town when a plane dropped on a school and restaurant; if our bus had been a minute sooner we would have been involved. We jumped out of the bus, and you could hear the children in the building screaming. Only six lived. Everyone in the restaurant was killed, including some American airmen. Seeing the devastation in the Persian Gulf on TV brings back many frightening memories. Hearing the air-raid sirens gives me a sick feeling in the pit of my stomach. One Saturday afternoon two German planes flew low down Main Street, strafing everything on the street. Many people were killed or maimed. No one knew how the planes got so far inland, and no one saw them coming across the border.

Harold came back to Grand Junction in October 1945. My son Paul and I reported to the camp in Tidworth for processing in January 1946. I was homesick for several years. I had left my family, friends and relatives, and knew we did not have the money for me to go home to visit. But after I finally made a trip to England in 1962, I seemed to settle down better to my life in America.

Hazel Fiegel
Grand Junction, Colorado

On The Line With TNT

When my husband left for the service, I knew I could not teach while he was gone. He wanted me to live with his parents in Fort Madison, Iowa. My first job was at a grocery store as a cashier. People don't realize how spoiled and selfish we are when it comes to sacrificing. There were many things we couldn't get at the store, such as Jell-O and marshmallows. We would keep some of the items that were short under the counter and give them to our best customers.

One day a lady and her husband came in. She asked for several of the items we didn't have. She said, "I'll be so glad when the War is over, and we can get these things again." I remarked, "I will also be glad. Then my husband can be home." A funny look came on her face. Her husband was by her side.

Later, I decided to go to work at the ordnance plant in Burlington, Iowa. I worked on the detonator line putting TNT pellets in the detonator. I worked on the line until my skin became yellow from the TNT. I decided to quit before it got into my system.

It was hard being away from my husband, but it made us stronger and more able to face many of the things life has dealt us. Praise the Lord he did come home, and we will soon be celebrating our 54th wedding anniversary.

Mildred Swinford
Keokuk, Iowa

WAC Enlistment Leads To Travel

I was 18 years old when the Japanese bombed Pearl Harbor. I lived on a farm in Illinois. One of my brothers served in the Army and one in the Navy. I served in the Women's Air Corps.

I was sent to New York City when the War was over in Europe to help with the mail. They were five months behind when we got there. We lived in the Hotel Herald Square with headquarters in the Hotel Collingwood. From there I went to Europe.

I left the United States on August 12, 1945, from Newport News, Virginia; the War was over August 14. We landed in France. After a few weeks in tents, we were sent to Vienna, Austria.

I worked as a telephone operator for about a year. I had worked as a telephone operator before enlisting as a WAC.

Gen. Mark Clark was commander of our area. His train was hooked to our switchboard when in Vienna. I received a Commendation Ribbon while in Vienna.

Armeda Jenness
Kingsley, Iowa

Santa In A Marine Uniform

In 1943, I took off from work at Continental Oil Company's home office, terribly sick. The county health doctor confirmed that I had a severe case of polio. I went to the quarantine ward of St. John's Hospital in Tulsa, Oklahoma. I spent six and one-half weeks there and eight months at home gaining enough strength to go back to work, which I did in the summer of 1944. I worked in payroll accounting until V-J Day.

I had heard of vocational rehabilitation grants for college. I applied and became a freshman at the University of Oklahoma.

My vivid experience came after classes let out for the Christmas holidays. The old south Navy base at Norman, Oklahoma, was still active as a separation center for Navy and Marine personnel. The base personnel and all the students were bent on going home for the first peacetime Christmas since before World War II.

I made an educated guess that the afternoon train north would be packed. I decided on the 10 p.m. train. As it turned out, it seemed the evening crowd waiting for the train was half the base and campus population. I had my old blue suitcase and was standing near the wall of the station. Polio had left me with an unreliable left knee, and I was seriously thinking of going back to my dorm and trying the next day.

All of a sudden, the biggest Marine sergeant I've ever seen came over to me and said, "Miss, you want on the train, right?"

I sort of stuttered, "Yes." He said, "I'll get you on it." He slung his sea bag over one shoulder, picked up my suitcase with that same hand, grabbed me with his other arm and elbowed our way onto the train. He deposited me on top of my suitcase in the aisle. When I turned to thank him, he had disappeared.

My dad was waiting on the platform at Ponca City. I told him of my rescue by the Marine sergeant.

He grinned and said, "Maybe it was Santa masquerading as a Marine."

Jane Curtis Waldroop
Norman, Oklahoma

Townspeople Believed To Be Spies

I was in the sixth grade when the War broke out. We had an art teacher who left in the middle of the night. She was a German spy. Our town was Hitchcock, Oklahoma; 235 residents lived there. She stayed at Dr. Bernett's home. No one knew what had happened to her. We were so shocked.

I lived on a farm with my parents and rode the bus to school. We saved our toothpaste tubes and all our cans. We cut the tops and bottoms out, placed the ends inside and smashed the can flat.

I had to go to the dentist one Saturday; I was 14 and had never been there before. Dad, being a farmer, had to buy things for the tractor. He said, "I guess you will be OK 'til I get back," and he left me alone in the dentist chair. A few weeks later we heard the FBI took the dentist away as a German spy. It's a good thing I didn't know until after my appointment.

Our boys finally came home. My brother was stationed in England. I married my husband after he came home from Guam. The one I was in love with was killed the first year on the Burma Road by the Japanese. They captured the boys under his command and killed him.

We were so glad when the War came to an end. I wish people would still love the good old United States.

Henrietta (Hiebert) Fleshman
Enid, Oklahoma

For One Hearty Meal

We were WAVE ensigns stationed at the 13th Naval District Headquarters in Seattle during World War II. We lived in a Women's Officer Quarters at the naval station where many Navy ships were berthed while awaiting orders or provisions. Our own WAVEs mess was not the best by a long shot — lots of starches, unappetizing stews and goulashes of questionable character.

We were required to turn in our ration stamps to the mess officer, since we belonged to that mess. How we all longed for a good hearty meal of red meat — a real rarity during wartime. We often ate at the Bachelor Officers Club on the naval station where the food was more appetizing. They catered to the men of our Navy. It was only natural that one would strike up acquaintances with some of these seafarers. On one occasion a group of us was seated at a large table at the Officers Club mess, and several fellows whom we had met before joined us. During dinner we learned that they were about ready to set sail. Someone suggested that we give them a "shoving off" party, so we started to make plans for a picnic at a local park. Heavens! How could we have a decent picnic when we didn't have ration stamps even for hot dogs? Since the picnic was such a good idea, a couple of the fellows told us not to worry. They would provide the "dogs"; we were to serve up the rest of the fixings.

We arrived at the picnic site at the prescribed time and started unpacking the food. Imagine our surprise when we opened up the box of "hot dogs" and found a T-bone steak for everyone. We started cooking these precious morsels with tender loving care, thoroughly savoring that delicious aroma. Shortly, several other picnickers came to our table and enjoyed the smell of our steaks. We were the envy of all these unlucky people, and I always felt bad that we did not have enough to share. I knew the feeling of wanting a return to the good old days when life was normal and one could dine on whatever appealed to him — and no ration stamps.

Cmdr. Evelyn N. (Dene) Sooy
U.S. Naval Reserve (Retired)
San Diego, California

War Leads To Married Women Teachers

When I began teaching school in 1934, my contract stated that if I got married, I lost my job. It was not until World War II began, causing a shortage of school teachers, that this discrimination ended. Married women teachers became more acceptable.

My husband and I were married in 1937. He had just bought a

Ford coupe, which was fine then. But our family soon grew to include three small boys. We needed a new car, but new cars were unavailable during World War II. The boys took turns riding on the shelf behind the two regular seats. We were all happy when we were able to purchase a new car.

Clarice Morrison
Coleridge, Nebraska

WAVE Officer Gets To Know Sailors

It was not long after V-J Day that it all started. Night watches were not new to me. As a WAVE officer in communications, I had spent my entire naval career working night, evening, and day shifts, on the top deck of the Administration Building.

But now that the Japanese had surrendered, there was less classified material coming through on the top deck, and the main communications room below was understaffed. The married WAVE officers were leaving the service, the men communications officers had not returned from overseas, and another watch officer was needed to supervise one of the crews. I was to be it.

I had not been around sailors much because of the caste system in the Navy. On the watch to which I was now assigned, I would be the only female on duty in the communications room for the evening and midwatches. Brady and Carruthers were the ones I worked closest with, because we were responsible for checking and routing all messages from the teletype and radio rooms. The boys in the back room did all the sending and receiving of messages, unless they came upon a problem — in that case, Brady did it.

One night when Brady and Carruthers had gone out to midnight chow, I had to go into the teletype room about a message. The teletype made so much noise the men did not hear me come in. They were having problems, and Duke and Behrens were swearing angrily.

When they saw me, they straightened up. Duke said, "I'm awfully sorry, ma'am. Please yell out before you come in here. We wouldn't intentionally use that kind of language in front of you for anything."

The other WAVE communication officers on the other watches and I bought a Christmas tree for the office. Ornaments were not to be had that year, so we made our own out of cardboard. The sailors helped us cover cardboard stars and wreaths with foil and even joined us in painting walnuts with nail polish.

Jean Ciavonne
Colorado Springs, Colorado

Dream Melts Away

The War was over, but rationing was not. We were longing for many things, red meat and creamery butter among them. We were sick to death of that colored oleo.

I had exchanged my Navy uniform for the uniform of a United Air Lines stewardess. I flew out of Seattle to Cheyenne, Omaha and Denver. Shortly after starting my new career, I was on a lay-over in Omaha. I noticed a sign claiming this city to be the Butter Capital of the United States. I ventured into a market and found that I could buy creamery butter without ration stamps. I promptly invested in two full pounds of butter and envisioned sharing it with several friends, which would move my popularity up a couple of powerful notches.

I stored my precious cargo in my regulation suitcase along with the few clothes that I felt necessary for an overnight stay. When the crew and I reached the airport to board our plane for returning to Seattle, we found our flight had been cancelled. We were told that we would return on the next available flight, in about two hours. We pulled out our books and magazines and began killing time. Someone moved our bags to a safe area so we did not have to worry about keeping them with us.

When our flight was called I grabbed my bag and started for the gate. A passenger agent ran after me and told me that something was dripping from my bag. When I opened it up, imagine my horror: my precious butter was soup. Someone had placed my bag near a heating vent. My nightie, extra uniform and underwear were a greasy mess — and my dreams of being a big heroine likewise melted.

Cmdr. Evelyn N. (Dene) Sooy
U.S. Naval Reserve (Retired)
San Diego, California

Star For A Day: A Brief Brush With Fame

The nearest I ever came to becoming a movie star — my one fleeting brush with fame — was during World War II. I was married by then, but Uncle Sam said to Bob, "I want you!" So, it was the Army Air Force for him: aircraft schools all over the United States and then off to the island of Saipan.

A year before Bob went overseas, I had answered an Emerson Electric want ad for training women to be draftsmen. I was trained at Hadley Technical School and began working in the West Florissant, Missouri, office of the Emerson Electric Turret Plant.

Being a woman draftsman was a far cry from the movie world, but the pay was much more than teacher's pay, and the work was almost as interesting. At least I felt that I was doing my bit for the country. The office itself was larger than any room I had ever seen in my life, and it was completely filled with draftsmen and engineers.

For those who are too young to know about turrets, they are gunner's enclosures on all fighter planes, which protected the breech portion of the gun. The breech is the part of the firearm at the rear of the bore. The bore is the interior tube of the gun. Some turrets were stationary, and some revolved.

The men with whom I worked were constantly designing and perfecting more types of turrets for warfare on Navy aircraft carriers and tanks. The ones the Emerson Plant turned out were turrets for bombers and fighter planes of all kinds.

One day I was working away at my drafting table when a little man with thick lenses surprised me. He said, "Mrs. Moffitt, how would you like to be in a movie?" I couldn't believe what I had heard; I couldn't speak. He said, "I mean it. We have picked you out of all the Emerson women to show off our turret designs. Will you come with me?

In a daze I followed him to his photo lab. He gave me a jumpsuit like the factory women had to wear every day. It fit perfectly, and when I came out he said, "Now, you look like an Emerson Electric worker."

It was my first time in the factory. The noise was overwhelming and I thought how great it was that I worked in a quiet office. It was very interesting to see the turrets come to life from drawings in which I had had a small part.

The photographer took me through the factory to a room with the finished product, their newest turrets. He filmed me at all angles with those monstrous things, and every time I smiled he barked, "Don't smile! This is serious business."

Other than the fact that I couldn't smile, the lights were hot, and my co-workers were teasing me about being a star, it was all great fun. But mainly, it was something exciting to write about to my husband.

I was always mystified about why a woman should be able to point out the parts and workings of a turret, but I never questioned the bosses, even when Stuart Symington, who was president of Emerson Electric at that time, told me the film was to be shown all over the world to every Allied airplane factory that planned to strengthen their country's defense.

Nelle Moffitt Allen
Redford, Missouri

CHAPTER 7: Over At Last

San Francisco Goes Wild

My mother was working in downtown San Francisco on V-J Day, when World War II ended. President Truman's announcement that Japan had surrendered came over the radio at 4 p.m. Pacific Standard Time, while most people were still at work. Early on, there was a report that a streetcar had been torn apart and set on fire on Market Street, so streetcars were no longer in operation east of Van Ness Avenue. Few people then drove "machines" to work, so it was a long walk for many.

Since Mother had been invited to have dinner at a friend's apartment on Nob Hill, she walked from work, coming very close to Chinatown. The Chinese had been at war with Japan for eight years, and they were elated that it was over. Many were shouting and throwing lighted strings of firecrackers. It was all very frightening. Two of the girls at dinner got mad at their boyfriends for flirting with girls in the window of an adjoining apartment, so for revenge, they leaned out of the front bay window and invited up every serviceman they saw! When the bell rang, they made one of the mothers answer and excuse their silliness. More than a dozen had answered the invitation!

At midnight they decided to go down to Market Street to see what was going on. The city was wild! One young woman bathed naked in the pool outside the Civic Center. Servicemen were everywhere. Some had broken into liquor stores and helped themselves. Display windows were broken, and men donned dresses, skirts and blouses they had taken off of the mannequins. Some climbed up to theater marquees and tore down the lettering of the current movies. Strangers hugged and kissed; some laughed, some cried. One sailor on crutches simply stood and cried. "My buddies didn't make it," he sobbed. About 5 a.m., Mother and her friends came upon an elderly lady sitting alone on a curb, singing loudly. She said that she had sons and grandsons overseas and had promised them that the minute the War was over, she would celebrate for them. And she did!

Many things went on in San Francisco that night — some funny, some very tragic. But there were nice things, too — friendliness and people helping and sharing with others. It was a lesson in human behavior.

Mother was one of the few who went to work the day after V-J Day, and since it had been declared a holiday, she received double pay. This event has remained forever vivid in her mind. Although she, too, was glad the War was over, Mother had enough of a sense of history to realize that she was in a special place, at a very special time.

Victoria Venditti
Lexington, Missouri

Wounds Run Deep

I was a child of 5 when my dad was drafted. He would be in the last or one of the last cavalry units to be trained at Camp Chaffee, Arkansas. They would later be called infantry.

There were two girls in my family, and before Daddy shipped out from Fort Ord, California, my brother was born. We lived in south central Kansas, not very far from both sets of grandparents.

My memories tend to be of the good and fun things; candy, starting to school, running errands and helping out with our new baby. Each home had a flag in their window with a star for each person in the service. Our flag only had one star, my grandmother's had two stars. My dad would be in the China, Burma and India Campaign. His brother was in the Pacific Theater. All those strange sounding names — Guam, Luzon, Midway, the Philippines, and of course, Hawaii.

I remember the hated ration stamps. I remember how we got word of the War by our battery-operated radio, if the battery was "up." The newspapers would usually be a day old when we got them, since we lived out in a country area.

I remember the V-mail and the censored, cutout letters that we got and how they looked so funny to us. There was always a page for us, and Mother would often cry when she read it to us. Mickey Rooney was in the same outfit as Daddy. I'm not sure how Mama got by, but she did, and there were always pennies for penny candy. There's no telling what she went without to buy our candy. And Danville was such a small town that it was as if we had dozens of grandparents.

A telegram came that daddy had been wounded in action. He was in a military hospital somewhere overseas, and would be shipped Stateside soon. It never said how badly he was wounded. I don't remember how long it was before we heard more, I only know that it seemed an eternity. I think he was in the hospital in California before we knew that his physical injuries were not bad. He had been shell shocked. It is called post-traumatic stress disorder now. It should be called "hell." He had been hauling supplies on the Burma Road and there was a major battle. He was one of two men who survived the battle, and since the other man was wounded seriously, he dragged him for three days 'til they were safe. The only physical injury my dad had was some scraps of shrapnel in his hand. There wasn't much help for this problem then.

Daddy was given a Purple Heart and was supposed to get another award, but he only wanted to forget all he could about that War. The hell he would often remember can never be imagined, unless you have seen one suffering as he did. He would re-live that battle, as we watched helplessly.

He used to be an avid sportsman and fisherman. Rabbit and squirrel hunting were his favorites. He would try to hunt, but he only used his guns for protection after a few tries. He had seen so many large snakes in the jungle that he was deathly afraid of the most harmless ones after he came home. He would leave fireworks displays, retreating to a distance where he wouldn't be able to hear. It would bring back the memories.

It certainly changed his life forever, and ours. He would carry those demons until the day he died in 1974.

His brother survived the battles of the Pacific Theater and returned home to be killed in a car wreck three years later.

One of his sisters married a man who had been severely wounded in France. It truly was a world war. I pray that it will never happen again.

My husband is a year older than me, but he can't remember that war at all. I told him that he would if his father had been in it like mine was. It wasn't over for our family when the peace treaty was signed, not even when my dad was buried. The memories are always there, burned in my heart forever.

Louise Parks
Bellflower, Missouri

Armistice: A Day To Remember

I have two memories that have stayed with me of World War II. At the time they happened I had no idea of what war was, as I was only 5 years old.

My aunt and uncle had moved in with us, and I enjoyed playing with my cousin, who was just a toddler. My aunt was so jolly and funny. I just loved being with her.

One day I heard laughter in the other room and went to investigate. My aunt was holding a little brown colored pill, looking at it closely. On the table below I saw what I thought was a bowl of lard. When I asked what it was, I was told it was a new kind of butter, called oleo. I didn't think I'd like it. My aunt could find no way to open it so she held it up as she stuck a pin in it. Everyone had a good laugh as the yellow fluid squirted all over.

Then came the day my dad bought me some new roller skates.

I was so proud of them. My dad was in front of the house showing me how to use the skates when I heard a lot of noise.

The streetcar a half-block down from our house had stopped. Windows opened, and people were laughing and crying. Dad started jumping up and down and yelling. I stood there ready to run. I was scared. "Dad, what's the matter?" I asked, starting to cry.

Dad replied, "The War's over, the Armistice has been signed!" I accepted the fact and went back to skating. I couldn't see what was so exciting.

It was a few years later before I understood what the Armistice was.

Evelyn Williams-Hall
Sioux City, Iowa

A World Opened Up

Before and during most of the war years I attended high school in a small Missouri town. This was mostly farm country with very little industry. I did not think my hometown was very exciting, and there certainly were very few chances for good employment.

I was the youngest of six girls, and while I was still in high school, one by one my sisters started looking for jobs. One worked in a 10-cent store, one in the office of a poultry-packing plant and one in the law office. The others married and moved away. Most of the jobs then only paid $5 a week, which wasn't much even back then. I remember baby-sitting for 10 cents an hour, and one summer I took care of a neighbor's three children, cleaned their house and cooked supper — all for the princely sum of $1.40 a week. With this money, my mother purchased material to make my school clothes.

Into this quiet little town the War suddenly exploded. A military air base was built in the country near our town. Now there were jobs to be had, and all of my sisters went to work for the base. A USO center opened in our town, which became filled with servicemen on weekends. It was heavenly to this teenage girl! All these handsome, lonesome boys flirted with us, whistled at us, dated, fell in love and even married many of the local girls. Some dance halls sprang up. At last there was a place to go and a lot of partners to dance with. This did not sit too well with our elders, but we young-uns loved it.

Upon graduation I was lucky enough to secure a job on the air base, too. My whole family moved out to live on the air base. All of us were now working for the government. The rent on the housing units was low; groceries could be purchased cheaply in the commissary. There was even a theater on the base, as well as weekly dances at the NCO or officer's clubs. The base was like a small town in itself. My salary was an unbelievable $25 a week. I was rich! All my old schoolmates thought I was the luckiest girl in the world.

All the men in our family had been called into service, and my poor mother would pace the floor night and day as each one was sent overseas. I can well remember the day FDR came on the radio announcing the bombing of Pearl Harbor — a day that would go down in infamy. Here we were: simple people, church-going people, learning first-hand about air raids, blackouts and the pain of separation from our loved ones. Other countries had always seemed far away from us, and now we were writing to and getting letters from all over the world as our servicemen were shipped out.

I must admit, being as young as I was I found it all terribly exciting. I thoroughly enjoyed all the activities on the base and being driven to and from work in a jeep by some of the servicemen I worked with.

There I was, a small town girl, meeting people from all over the United States, hearing exotic, foreign sounding names and all kinds of accents so different from our slow, Southern drawl. Why, we even had German prisoners of war at this camp. They worked on rubbish pick-up detail, and they would look through the trash and excitedly talk among themselves. One of the drivers who could speak German told me they could not believe the good things Americans threw away, things that would have been much valued in their country.

Strangely, we were never afraid of these prisoners, and all of them seemed like nice boys. They never treated us as if we were their enemies either. We were all just people.

Like most young people, I avoided the news on the radio, not wanting to hear or think about all the battles going on in Europe and the South Pacific. My brother was on one of the islands and sent me a silk-embroidered handkerchief from there, which I still have carefully stored away. There was the pinch of rationing for shoes, meat and gasoline. I still have a couple of ration stamps that I found in an old wallet belonging to my mother. As for shoes, we never had more than two pairs at one time, even when the War wasn't on. We didn't have a car, so gas rationing was no problem. Since we had always lived sparingly, rationing did not bother us as much as it did a lot of other people.

Had I been aware that the boy I was to marry years later was involved in all the military landings, shipwrecked at sea and experiencing untold hardships that would affect his health the rest of his life, I could not have been as carefree as I was. Yes, those were happy years for many of us. Talking to people in later years I found that those years had made such an impression — be it happy or sad — that their lives forevermore seemed to revolve around that time and their experiences.

I do hope there will never again be such a war. However, I must acknowledge the fact that the War did bring people closer together; it allowed people from many places to know one another. Many people were relocated far from their families, and they never came back to their hometowns to settle down. For the first time, people seemed to realize that there actually was a big world out there; many of the returning servicemen decided to look further than their home towns for a place to work and live. Young brides, who met their husbands on military bases far from home, chose to return to their husbands' home states after the War. They had learned to be independent and survive on their own; they no longer felt the need to stay close to family and familiar places.

Looking back, I suppose you could say that for some of us it was the best of times. For others it was the worst of times, but it was a time in this country that will never be forgotten by all of us.

We all had to grow up and live with the aftermath of the War. Many men, such as my husband, were robbed of their youth, their health broken. All of this took a great toll, but I never heard any of them regret what they did for their country. They all retained full patriotism and love for this great country of ours, and would have done battle again if called upon.

My good husband died much too young from complications of his war years, so it is very difficult for me to watch pictures about the War or read stories of war experiences without being terribly saddened. Sad for that girl who was so full of life and fun during those years, sad for my friends who did not return home, sad for the men whose lives were shortened by the effects of the War.

It was indeed the best and the worst of times.

> Helen Ward O'Key
> Litchfield, Connecticut

A Wartime Love Story

My boyfriend was drafted before I graduated from high school. We considered ourselves just good friends at the time he entered the Army. We wrote letters and exchanged thoughts on his training, my graduation and the War.

Seven months after he left for Army training, he came home on a short leave. During this leave we both knew our chemistry was saying, "This relationship is more than good friends, it's love." We agreed to continue our friendly relationship on these terms.

Fritz had a war to win, and I had a lady's life to live; we were not going to be tied down. Our future together was only going to be after the War, if things worked out that way for us.

Fritz went overseas to New Guinea and the Philippines, having rough battles on a landing boat. I was employed at home in Washington, D.C. Our letters continued — lots of them.

We both wanted the war to end. We were lonely and in need of seeing each other. The War did come to an end. That was a happy day. Fritz and I ended our separation three days short of three years. We were married six weeks after he returned home.

Myrtle May Duin
George, Iowa

Witness To History

Albert Dale Fecht fought in World War II. This is one of the stories he told.

Albert was assigned to overseas duty aboard the light cruiser *Pasadena*, which prowled the Pacific Ocean for 10 consecutive months. It steamed into Tokyo Bay V-J Day, September 2, 1945. The *Pasadena* anchored beside the warship *Missouri* to witness the signing of the surrender.

Every available topside area was crowded with men in freshly laundered whites who were eager for this long-awaited occasion. With a strange mixture of emotions, the men watched as the small figures of the Japanese surrender emissaries climbed the gangway and were piped aboard the *Missouri* for formal ceremonies on this historic day.

The *Pasadena* arrived back into the United States January 19, 1946.

The Red Cross had a message for Albert. It was: "Your father is ill, come home immediately." Albert boarded a train for Tribune, Kansas. Friends were waiting for him. They found his father at a gas station, all bent over, and very ill.

Albert put his father in a vehicle and sped the 34 miles to the nearest hospital before going home.

His father's appendix had burst in three places; it had been that way for three days.

Albert was discharged from the Navy in April 1946.

Submitted by Pauline Fecht
Syracuse, Kansas

Poem For Mother

My mom was a true mother
and always a friend.
We spent many hours talking
and walking hand-in-hand.
She loved all her children,
seven are alive.
One baby went to heaven;
he prays in the sky.
Mom had six children
through the second World War,
the bombs were falling
and we were small.
She was all alone with six little kids,
only God saw her weeping
as he watched in her sleep.
Soon the War was over
and spring came to our land.
My father and brother came home again.
It was Palm Sunday
and Easter they returned.
We all went to church
and sang God's praises again and again.

Theresa M. Herzig
Towaco, New Jersey

The Fatted Lamb

As World War II drew to a close, my husband and I were married. Being married to a serviceman allowed my children and me to travel overseas to his duty stations.

When we arrived in southern Italy, scars of the bombing there were very visible. Americans were not especially welcome at that particular time.

We lived a few blocks from the NATO Command. Our young children and I would walk to the military facility for some of our needs. We would pass the ground-level apartment of an Italian family; the kitchen door was almost always open.

Several weeks before Easter, we saw a lamb being raised behind the kitchen stove, which was directly in line with the open door. The floor of the apartment was earth.

The lamb grew larger each passing week.

The week after Easter, instead of seeing the lamb behind the stove we saw the sheepskin nailed on the outside of the house drying. We imagined the family enjoyed the fatted lamb for Easter dinner.

This was a little difficult to explain to our small children.

Helen L. Bean
Wayne, Nebraska

Veterans Receive Low Priority

From the time that my husband Wilton left, until he arrived home, he was gone more than three years. We wrote lots of letters and shed many a tear.

The War ended on my birthday, September 2, 1945. Wilton was stationed in Shanghai, China, on board the repair ship the *USS Oceanious.*

We were hoping he would be home by Christmas. His two brothers were already home, one from Europe and the other from the Pacific. On December 15, 1945, he arrived in California.

The servicemen hoped upon hope to be home. No such luck. He called to say that it would be after Christmas. The civilians had priority on travel over the servicemen and women because the government would not pay as much for the fare. We felt it wasn't fair for the servicemen who had fought for our country to wait because of civilians traveling home for Christmas.

Mildred Swinford
Keokuk, Iowa

Love Letters

World War II was the incident that put my family-to-be together. It was January 1, 1944, when a young Oklahoma soldier stationed in Biloxi, Mississippi, wrote his first letter to a young Kansas girl, asking if she would correspond with him. His married brother, who was an acquaintance of this girl, was the instigator of his action. His letter was answered, which marked the beginning of a long-distance courtship.

The young soldier soon left for overseas duty, where he served in England and Holland with the 57th Fighter Control Squadron of the U.S. Air Force. Through the discouraging, encouraging, lonely and sweet letters that followed, they fell in love with each other, sight unseen.

After one year and nine months of letters flying over the Atlantic Ocean, and the surrender of Germany, the Liberty Ship carrying this young soldier made a sudden route change. Instead of going to Hawaii, where it was headed, the ship turned and headed home to the good ol' United States. The moment was about to arrive when the young soldier would meet his dream girl for the first time. Would either of them be disappointed? Was all this correspondence in vain?

In September of 1945 the young soldier walked into the U.S. Post Office where the girl of his dreams worked. Her little sister was standing in front of the post office, peeking from behind a light pole to see what would transpire. Each recognized the other from exchanged photos, and both acted as though they weren't strangers at all. The other postal employees never knew this to be their first meeting.

Six months later they were married. Now, 47 years down the road, they have six children and eight grandchildren, with another on the way. Thanks to World War II, I had this young soldier and his dream girl for my mom and dad.

Floyd Elliott
Grand Junction, Colorado

Much To Be Thankful For

During World War II, I worked for Coors Porcelain Company in Golden, Colorado. I had married an Air Force sergeant, and he was sent overseas, as were so many of my girl friends' husbands. With gas rationing as it was, a group of us on paydays would ride the streetcar into Denver, eat at a nice restaurant, go to a movie, then ride the streetcar back home.

My most memorable day was on Thanksgiving 1945. I was entertaining my family and in walked my husband, unexpected. What a Thanksgiving memory.

Theresa Stingerie Bainbridge
LaSalle, Colorado

True Love Returns

Ferdie and I were not married when World War II started. But we were in love; he gave me my engagement ring on one of his furloughs home.

The days he was in the Army were long and lonesome, but our letters helped. We planned our future home via our letters, knowing that someday we would live in it together. He drew the floor plans; I added details such as, "a white house with a blue roof."

Many friends were getting sad news about their loved ones. I was concerned about Ferdie's safety too, of course, and prayed for him night and day.

He was wounded in the fighting in Germany. He was sent to France and then England for healing and therapy. Then back to the front. He was sent all over Europe trying to find his company, or one that could use him.

It was a frustrating time. He moved so often that he never had an address to send me so that I could keep writing to him. I wrote almost every day. He received some of them in bunches. The rest eventually found their way back to my parents' home months after we were married.

Heartbreaking letters went to some of my friends: "I don't love you any more," or "I'm not waiting for you." Never once in all those years of waiting and uncertainty did I doubt Ferdie's love and faithfulness. There would never be a "Dear Jane" letter for me.

The first year Ferdie was gone, I worked as assistant to the postmaster in the little town of Iliff, Colorado. There I learned the importance of letters to other people. When someone received a letter from their special serviceman or woman, it was opened immediately in the post office waiting room. Both good and bad news was shared with us; we kept up with what was happening to the young people in Uncle Sam's service who were from our community.

It was months after the War was over before Ferdie finally got home. I'd quit my job three months previously to stay home with Mother and Daddy and do some sewing for my hope chest.

Ferdie had decided he was not going to be a casualty of war nerves — mental or emotional. He didn't like to talk about the War; and he didn't — the really bad parts anyway. He sometimes told of interesting or humorous incidents. Neither did he want to meet and become friendly with any other ex-servicemen. "They're all crazy or liars," he said. Then he'd do or say something goofy to prove his point.

There were a few times, though, when he'd wake up at night and think he heard someone outside. He'd take the flashlight and go all around the house checking — remembering, I'm sure, what night noises had meant not too long before.

Mary Ann Kunselman
Longmont, Colorado

Coming Home

My memories about World War II center around my Uncle Herbert Nelson's homecoming. My parents, my baby sister, my mother's slightly retarded brother and I lived in a tiny town, a place in the road really — called Dover, Florida. Our house was built with the back facing a long dirt road; on the other side were the piney woods and palmettos. This road led to the highway where my father walked each morning to catch his ride to work.

We were about a half mile from the nearest neighbors, and the land was situated so that one could look down the road toward the highway and see anyone walking in the direction of our home.

One sunny morning, Mama was doing yard work, and I was playing nearby. I did not see anyone coming, and neither did my mother. Suddenly, a tall, thin man in an Army uniform came striding down the dirt driveway toward my mother. Dropping her gardening tools, she made a small cry and ran to the man. They embraced and cried and smiled at the same time.

I might have been frightened, since I was a shy child, but somehow I was not. I walked closer and stared up at my mother, who looked down and said, "This is your Uncle Herbert. He's been away in the War." I was 4 years old, and this was the first I knew about an Uncle Herbert. He had come to stay a while and would share a room with his younger brother at the end of the house.

Uncle Herbert bought a Model A Ford with his mustering-out pay, and we proudly rode to the crossroads grocery store and to the Baptist Church. Mama said the car sounded like a sewing machine. He often drove us to see relatives in nearby towns. Once my sister and I were playing on the edge of a fish pond, the kind people used to have in their front yards for decoration or landscaping. The deep end was about three feet deep, and Sissy fell in. I screamed and groped under the water. I couldn't swim and was afraid to go in. I got her dress and pulled her up as everyone came running out. Uncle Herbert asked me if I pushed her. He had seen me hit her with a swing at another time and was suspicious. But that time the fall was an accident.

My uncle had never married and was not used to young children. He would hold me on his lap sometimes, and I often asked him to do this. He was very nervous from the War and would jump visibly if someone dropped silverware. I began to drop mine just to see him jump, until Mama got wise and spanked me hard for it.

I was a timid child and easily disciplined. However, my sister, who was only a year and one-half old and very precocious, got the idea to crawl under the dining table and bite Uncle Herbert's leg. She did this several times, until he asked my mother if it would be all right to bite Sissy back. My mother gave permission, and the next time, Uncle picked Sissy up and bit her on the leg. Did she ever howl! She was a very quick learner and did not bite anyone's leg after that.

The thing I remember as the most outstanding change he made in my life was a little red toothbrush. I don't know why my mother had not taught me to brush my teeth yet. Uncle Herbert looked surprised when she admitted this fact. He went to town and bought me a little red toothbrush and a small carton of Arm & Hammer baking soda. Then he took me to the back porch, where there was a sink and pump, and showed me how to brush my teeth. He told me I should do this morning and evening.

My favorite Christmas memory came during this time. We had an aunt and several older cousins who lived about a mile down the road. While I was eating supper, my cousin Gladys came in very quietly and put gifts under the pine tree, lit the fire in the fireplace and strung red and green ribbons across the ceiling. Everyone said Santa Claus came while I was eating. One of the gifts was a small clothesline, wooden pins and doll clothes to wash and hang out.

After about a year of my uncle living in our rather small house, things became a little strained. My uncle decided to find employment on one of the nearby farms and move out. He took his brother with him and was responsible for Uncle Orman from then on. He was very thrifty and was able to save enough to buy his own small farm and orange grove. He also bought a new tractor and an almost-new pickup truck.

As I grow older, I wonder about his talent for stretching money so far. Some people cannot handle a good salary, but he took a small amount and made it work for him and his brother.

Uncle Herbert became a member and deacon in the Baptist Church. He was a most religious man, living his religion and not just talking it. He did not marry. After Uncle Orman died, Uncle

Herbert lived alone, and when he passed on, he left his estate to the Baptist Church. I am very glad to have shared part of my life with this man. To me, he was just as courageous after the War as he had been in the War.

Dora De Shong
Aubrey, Texas

A World Forever Changed

When the War ended and the boys came home, many were disabled. Too many just didn't return. This was the start of a new era and a new structure for family life. The war effort was the first time so many mothers went to work outside the home, the first time so many children were unsupervised. Divorce became the answer to problems that could not be worked out with some war-torn families. Many children were without fathers. The War changed our world forever.

Desoree Thompson
Beaumont, California

Some Of Us Stayed Home

During World War II, each had a job to do. My job was to stay home and take care of two great little boys. One was 3 years old, the other, 2. Their daddy had joined the Navy. So many of his friends who were single had been gone for two years or more.

The three of us had some great times, and some scary.

Grandpa had given the boys a magnet. They were having fun with it, until the 2-year-old swallowed a small piece of metal they had found. It had four sharp corners. Of course, it hurt going down. I gave him some bread to eat. Although I was a nurse, I decided to phone the one doctor left in our area. He said, "Good, and give him some raw apple." All the time I was talking to the doctor, this scared baby sitting beside me kept asking, "Am I going to heaven?" I can still see those big blue eyes searching my face. A day later — with some pain — he passed the piece, much to my relief. We walked to Grandpa's place of business. The older boy threw open the door and announced to all, "He grunted and we got the metal."

Another time the older boy, who was 4 by then, came to me crying. He was shaking and crying so hard that I had to calm him first. He finally told me, "I put a pretty rock up my nose." I could see it, but not remove it. I told him to listen to me and do as I told him. Breathe in your mouth like Mommy is doing. Close your mouth, and blow through your nose. Repeating this several times, until he understood, we recovered the pretty rock. Tears were dried and there were lots of hugs.

Taking them to town was exciting for them, and kept me busy. One day at the local A&P store they accidentally broke a bottle of ammonia. They knew they were in trouble. I can still see them standing side-by-side, watching me and the manager clean it up.

One night I was awakened by the sound of breaking wood. I crept downstairs. The sound was coming from the basement. Listening, I wondered why our small dog Tiny wasn't alerted. I slowly opened the door and switched on the light. Soon the breaking of wood resumed. Creeping to the landing, I could see this small dog breaking the wood with his mouth and teeth. The boys had put him in a banana box. Much relieved, I helped him out. I laughed to myself about this burglar in the night. Indeed I laughed many times about their mischievous doings, never letting them know.

I dressed them in their navy blue coats with the gold buttons and their real sailor caps sent by Daddy and took them down to the railroad tracks one block away. The troop trains stopped here to take on water. The troops — especially the sailors — would cheer and wave to the boys. These young men hanging out the windows probably had children or brothers left at home. I felt sad at times, because besides my husband, I too had two young brothers in the Navy.

Two and one-half years later, their father returned. The older one had started to school. He had become listless and ill; he could not understand why Daddy wasn't coming home. He knew that other men had returned. One day Grandpa brought the mail and a box of his daddy's belongings — that convinced him that Daddy really was coming. Was he happy! He got up and started eating and was himself again. The younger brother didn't remember his daddy. He was suspicious of this stranger. It took a while for him to accept this person. Tiny, our big protector, didn't like this man either. In fact, he nipped at his heels more than once.

Now we were four again, beginning a new life.

Dorothy F. Eichhorn
Brooklyn, Iowa

Of War and Valentines

"Hello!" a feminine voice said excitedly, "Hello, Johnny!" and I turned with an expectant feeling of happiness. This was the first voice except Mama's that had greeted me by name in the two hours since my arrival home after four years of enduring the travail of war. It was St. Valentine's Day, and my mind was focused on thoughts of the gift I had come downtown to buy for my girl.

As I glanced casually at the speaker, I froze momentarily, for the face before me was not in my memory bank. In fact, it was so unnaturally beautiful my immediate reaction was one of rejection. Looking into set blue eyes, lovely but expressionless lips and smooth, porcelainlike skin, an uneasy feeling stirred in the pit of my stomach.

All too slowly, my eyes took in a perfect cheek and brow such as I had never seen before. This was not a human face, but a mask. A strange, beautiful, doll-like mask.

"Hello....?" I queried, sincerely hoping I had managed to suppress a momentary recoil. Sensing failure, I made a weak attempt at smiling as the girl turned swiftly away from me.

"Nice to see you home, Johnny," she murmured before hurrying on, huddled in a bulky coat against the cold winds of February.

Just after dinner that evening, Mama drew me aside. I sensed there was something on her mind, and I welcomed a discussion to relieve me of the shadow of my afternoon encounter.

"Johnny," Mama said slowly, "I've wanted to talk to you ....about Marie."

"Marie," I laughed inwardly with a warm feeling of relief. Marie was my girl. The girl of all my days. The girl who had seen me through a war of unbelievable cruelty and misery. As a nurse, she had followed me into battle and spent her courage consoling me across the world. Thoughts of her had helped me survive long months of imprisonment.

I could only grin with happiness. Leave it to Mama to choose just the subject that would erase all wayward thoughts. I spoke her name again, "Marie."

Then I said, "You know, Mama, I've been saving Marie for tonight. My special Valentine!"

"Johnny..." Mama's voice was laced with emotion, "About Marie... There's something we should have told you months ago..."

Mama's voice droned on... "Bombs... shell fragments... miracles... plastic surgery..." These were words I didn't need to hear. I knew them and was sick with remembering.

I remembered my girl on a bomb-ridden Pacific Island. My girl's letters written from a lonely hospital base. Just routine duty, she had said. But most of all, I could hear my girl's voice this afternoon saying excitedly, "Hello! Hello, Johnny!"

Marie ... oh, Marie! My one dear love!

Sara Hewitt Riola
Lakewood, New Jersey

Loss Of A Great Leader

On April 12, 1945, President Roosevelt died. That was one of the saddest days during World War II. The government offices were closed, and we were sent home. We sat in our rooms and listened to the commentators and funeral music on the radio.

All of Washington lined Constitution Avenue to watch the caisson carrying Roosevelt's casket pulled by six white horses. The caisson was followed by a riderless horse with a saddle and boots placed backwards in the stirrups. Everyone was mourning Roosevelt's death. Could the war be won without our leader?

Later, President Roosevelt's body was taken to Hyde Park and buried in the garden. Vice President Truman was sworn in as President, and the War continued.

Toward the end of August 1945 we were told the Bureau of Ships was not allowing any more contracts. Work slowed down, but we were told to look busy. Every time the loud speaker in our building sputtered, we expected the end of the War to be announced. This continued for at least a month. On September 1, 1945, I had just arrived home from work in the afternoon, when the announcement came over the radio. Japan had signed the peace treaty.

Everyone headed for downtown Washington. People were hanging on the outside of the streetcars. There were conga lines up and down F and G Streets. Ticker tape was hanging from the upstairs office windows on F Street.

Servicemen went up and down the streets kissing every pretty girl they saw.

My friends and I walked across the Ellipse to the White House. President Truman and Bess came out on the balcony and waved to the milling crowd.

Everyone came to work the next morning with broad smiles on their faces. World War II was over!

Soon, civil service workers were being laid off, and we said goodbye to our many friends and acquaintances.

We had made friends from all parts of the United States and gained a vast knowledge of the U.S. capital and Congress. It was an experience that enriched our lives and one that we would never forget.

Beatrice Sanders
Los Lunas, New Mexico

A Special Day Indeed

V-J Day was a completely different type of celebration. People milled through the streets, shouting and elated. A dance band played, and people who hadn't danced for years got out and danced.

A prominent citizen had saved some fireworks from the pre-war days. He fired sparklers, roman candles and all kinds of noise makers from the roof of the library. For those whose men were safe, it definitely was a time to rejoice — but for the survivors, it was a tragedy.

One man had made the boast that he would lead the high school band down the street in his boxer shorts if his son came home unharmed.

Everyone wondered if he would fulfill his boast, and people laughed at such a brag. All of a sudden, the sound of the band was heard in the distance. There he was, wielding the baton. He wore his boxer shorts, which were partly covered by a white shirt.

It was a time for revelry; little thought went to the boys who gave their lives for their country.

Now was the time for American soldiers to breathe easier and rebuild their lives.

Many GIs came home with problems, but for the most part, they survived pretty well. No family was without problems if the man of the house had been absent for a long time.

Madonna Storla
Postville, Iowa

Mantrap Trips Returning Husband

When my husband, Harold, was in the Army, I took my babies by train and went to live with my mother in Pennsylvania while he was in the service.

When the War was over, Harold returned home in the middle of the night. Mother was having a new foundation put under her house. It was all dug out around two sides, and the house was up on jacks.

It was raining hard when Harold got off the bus along the highway near Mother's house. He decided not to knock on the front door, which would awaken Mother.

He came around the house to my bedroom window. Just as he raised his hand to tap on my window, down he went into the cellar. He was a muddy mess! He accused me of having a mantrap under my window.

Alice R. Mason
Toledo, Iowa

Unexpected Help

I returned home in 1946, after almost four years in the Army. The experiences I had left me bitter with the world. I had decided I would stop to visit Mom and Dad before going on to a big city to live. I wasn't in the mood for working. I was going to join the 52-20 club. The government was paying the veterans $20 a week for up to 52 weeks while adjusting to civilian life. I was aiming for the full amount.

My brother had come home after serving almost four years in England and purchased one of the grocery stores in a small northwest Kansas town. His meat cutter suddenly quit to go to Oregon. I agreed to help him out for a few weeks. After I was there about six weeks, my brother left for the day. When he came back he told me he had a job and was leaving the store.

I asked, "Who's going to buy the store?"

He replied, "You are!"

I said, "With what? I don't have a hundred dollars to my name."

A few evenings later I was in the local tavern with a friend who always bought the beer for us. He asked me, "What are you going to do about buying the store?"

I said, "Nothing. I talked to the banker about a loan and he told me, 'I won't loan you any money on the store. It is too risky. If you were buying cattle, I would make you a loan.' It looks as if I will be out of a job."

He asked, "How much money would you need to buy it?" I told him the figure.

As the evening went on I was visiting with a man next to me. My friend was busy writing a check, which I thought was for more beer money. He tore the check out and nudged me in the ribs, and when I turned around he handed me the check. I said, "What is this?"

He said, "Look at it." I looked and was astonished to see that it was for the amount I needed to buy the store.

He would not draw up a promissory note: he said he knew I would pay him back. He was a friend indeed.

Ivan French
Mercedes, Texas

Making The Most Of Time

My first realization that we were at war in World War II was when some of the boys in our high school class of 1940 quit school and enlisted. You hear about war, but until someone you know or love is involved in it, it doesn't have much of an impact.

We had the usual U.S. bond drives, blackouts and air-raid drills, even though I lived in a small town.

While working at J. C. Penneys in 1941 and '42, there were shortages of silk hose, denim overalls and many other things.

I met my husband, Bob Holmes, in 1943 while he was stationed at Fitzsimmons Hospital in the medical corps. In May of 1944 we were married in Chicago, his home town, during a five-day delay before he left for the European Theater of War. The next day he left on his extended tour of duty, and I returned to my home in Paonia to await his return.

Those days and months were long, lonely and sad. Many of my letters from my husband were censored and parts of them cut out. If he wanted anything sent to him I had to show his letter of request to the postmaster before they would accept the package. Sometimes he wanted cheese and crackers, but mostly letters and pictures from home. I tried to write every day. I became very frustrated and frightened when I didn't get a letter — sometimes for weeks — but now I know when you're fighting a war and on the move, you don't always have time for letter writing.

While my husband was in Germany, he stayed briefly with a glass blower's family. He sent me a wine decanter and two beautiful wine glasses that this glass blower had given him. He also saw the German people rolling large wheels of cheese down the road, probably to a market.

When he returned to the United States he had a 30-day delay en route to the South Pacific. It was in Chicago that we heard the news of the bombing of Hiroshima and the end of the War. I shed many tears that day; first, for the ones who would never come home and their families; next, tears of joy that my husband did come home safely to me. Even though many war-time marriages didn't last, we've been married almost 47 years, and we praise the Lord for these years together.

Carrie Holmes
Grand Junction, Colorado

Waiting Out The War

We lived in Sibley, Iowa, a county seat of 3,000. In a small park, a wooden billboard was erected, bearing the names of every county man and woman in the service. I often stopped there to admire my brothers' names and to see whose name had been added to the list.

Displayed in parlor windows were red, white, and blue banners, with a star for each member of the household in the service. A family across the street from us earned a Gold Star banner when their son died in action.

When that happened, I heard that if someone died in the war the family received money — an insurance payment. The figure

$10,000 comes to mind now, but I don't know if that is correct. At any rate, it was more money than my siblings and I could comprehend, and we were intrigued with the possibilities of what it would buy for our large family. In a game akin to Truth or Dare, we asked one another, "Which would you rather have, Joe and Vince, or the money?" No one, of course, dared admit wanting the money. The answer was always that we would rather have our brothers safely back home than any amount of money — a million, billion or trillion dollars.

We asked Ma "the question," and her disapproving look told us we had better never ask it again. She said that no amount of money would make up for losing her sons. Maybe, as young as we were, we knew that. After all, we had never chosen the money. At some point, we figured out that since our brothers were married the payment would go to their widows. That ended any speculation — unspoken, of course — on what we might do with a sudden fortune.

Happily, my brothers survived the war, but during their absence our family suffered losses on the home front. In 1943, a 15-year-old daughter died from kidney disease, and in 1945 an infant son died from pneumonia.

My most vivid memory of the War's end is one in which my sister-in-law Iris, who lived with us, was reading a letter from her husband, my oldest brother. "He's coming home — Joe's coming home next week," she yelled to the rest of us, then devoured the rest of the letter privately.

A popular song was playing on the radio: *"Kiss me once, and kiss me twice, and kiss me once again. It's been a long, long time."* Smiling broadly, her big brown eyes aglow, Iris said, "It sure has been a long, long time."

That seemed to say it all. It had been a long, long time; for anxious family members waiting at home, and for the men and women overseas. But with my brothers coming home, the war was really over for our family.

Madonna Dries Christensen
Sarasota, Florida

A Little Bit Of Home

Our little country church was a small one, average attendance counting children was about 50. Our young people were busy in the war effort, taking the place of the young men who were on the front lines around the world.

Our pastor was a young family man with four children. We set up a weekly letter-writing system to all of the servicemen who were members' friends and kin. We had 77 on our list. Sister Friend, the pastor's wife, wrote a sermonette each week, which we typed and hectographed copies to send each one. We also drew names among the members and mailed a personal letter to each serviceman; some would write to four or five boys every week.

Brother Friend made a nice letter holder and put it in the church for replies we might receive from our soldier boys. All could read them who wished. Every service — and individually through the week — we prayed for all the soldiers.

God was gracious, and everyone on our list returned home without a disabling injury. Only one boy in our community lost his life. His family attended another church and we missed getting him on our list. We still thank God for keeping our boys safe on all the front lines of the battlefronts around the world.

Mayoma E. Bennett
Canton, Oklahoma

Wedding Dress From A Silk Parachute

From an article in *The Madison Daily Leader*, Madison, South Dakota, November 11, 1993.

Gordon Gerling of Rutland (South Dakota) brought home a Japanese silk parachute from his experience in the War. Gerling's experience began on August 14, 1945 — V-J Day. He and his 3,000 comrades left San Francisco on board a troop ship that day. They all believed they would be turned around to come home, because the War was officially over. They weren't turned around, and in fact went to the Philippines, where 1,000 of them split off into the

32nd Division also called the Red Arrow Division. Gerling was among them as a medic.

They were sent to a Japanese port, then took a one-day train trip to Yamaguchi where they were to be stationed. While they were there, Gerling was assigned to be the driver for a captain who was also a doctor. One of the captain's friends somehow acquired a Japanese silk parachute, which ultimately came to the unit in which Gerling was serving. The unit decided to use the parachute as part of their holiday decorations, so they draped it behind the Christmas tree.

After the holiday leave, the unit members decided to have a drawing for the parachute. Gerling was told that his name had been drawn to receive the parachute.

The parachute was sent home to Gerling's mother in Lemars, Iowa, where it stayed until Gerling and his fiance Shirley Herzig began preparing for their wedding after the War.

Gerling suggested to his bride-to-be that she might use the silk of the white parachute to make her wedding dress. Mrs. Gerling said, "I was honored that he suggested using the parachute to make my dress. It was something special from Gordon's time in the service so it was wonderful for me to get to share in that."

Mrs. Gordon Gerling
Rutland, South Dakota

INDEX